SEASONS OF FAITH

A Spiritual Anthology

Prepared by

Students, Faculty, Staff, Alumni, and Friends

of Walla Walla College

1999

Editor: Terrie Aamodt
Managing Editor: Kimberly Eley
Cover and divider page design: Aiko Tomita
Page layout: Tori Carroll

Cover type: Enya
Body type: Palatino and Sanvito

Printed using Computer-to-Plate Technology with QuarkXPress desktop publishing software

Printed by Pacific Press® Publishing Association, Nampa, Idaho

Acknowledgements

This book began when a lot of people took up an invitation to share the deepest part of their spiritual life—a joyous, courageous gift.

Nancy Cross and a host of helpers conducted a workshop that refined writers' ideas and dispelled shyness.

Three wise, insightful folk read all the manuscripts (minus author names) and chose the ones that shape this book: Dan Lamberton, professor of English; David Thomas, pastor of the College Place Seventh-day Adventist church and member of the college's Board of Trustees; and Helen Thompson, professor emeritus of English.

Kim Eley, senior English major, tracked all of the manuscripts through the process and kept a multitude of details organized; Colette deHaan, senior English major, lent typing and proofreading assistance; Marcie Wombold alchemized a stack of manuscripts into compatible computer files. Janice Dopp's sharp proofreading eyes read the evolving pages over and over. Linda Andrews lent her copy editing skills and "fresh eyes."

Tom Emmerson's commercial art class contributed many creative ideas for the book, and Aiko Tomita carried her concept through to the final design. Linda Nelson's graphic design class yielded the patience and expertise of Tori Carroll, who transformed the typed pages into a book.

Bev Beem unerringly spotted the ideal texts for the divider pages.

Tom Emmerson, Dan Lamberton, and Linda Nelson went the second mile (and beyond) for this project.

W. G. Nelson, Walla Walla College president, encouraged the enterprise and literally made it possible.

The result is a collective prayer and a spiritual gift—to you.

—Terrie Aamodt, editor

Table of Contents

The poor and needy search for water,
    but there is none; their tongues
    are parched with thirst.

But I the Lord will answer them;
    I, the God of Israel,
    will not forsake them.

I will make rivers flow
    on barren heights,
    and springs within the valleys.

I will turn the desert
    into pools of water, and the
    parched ground into springs.

I will put in the desert
    the cedar and the acacia,
    the myrtle and the olive.

I will set pines in the wasteland,
    the fir and the cypress together,

So that people may see and know,
    may consider and understand,

That the hand of the Lord
    has done this, that the
    Holy One of Israel has created it.

Isaiah 41:17-20, NIV

A Nudge in Time

Bruce Johnston

JOHNSTON KILLED IN ARGUMENT screamed the
Sunday paper. To the eyes and mind of a seven-year-old, it
didn't register. But when mother called my brother, sister
and me together to tearfully tell us that Daddy wouldn't
ever come home again, it hit me in the stomach like a bolt
of lightning. It couldn't be. Not my beloved Dad. Dad,
who was my best friend. Dad, whose smile was
contagious. Dad, who laughed and made life seem worth
living. Dad, who responded to Mr. Hodgkin's question
when we rolled into his Shell station in the Model T, "Who
is that you have with you, Bud?" "Oh, that's the man who
crossed the English Channel on a raft of crowbars." Boy,
did that make me feel like somebody (though I had not the
foggiest notion what or where the English Channel was, to
say nothing of the impossibility of crossing it on a raft of
crowbars). But I knew that Dad was my pal and that,
though I was just a little kid, the "baby" of the family, the
runt of the litter, so to speak, I was important to him. Yes,
Dad was an alcoholic. Yes, I knew what it was to fear his
steps when he came home drunk from the saloon. But that
was only on Saturday nights. The rest of the week he was
my hero.

A gregarious man widely known and loved, a veteran
of the Spanish American War, his health ravaged by the
diseases contracted in the jungles of the Philippines in
1898, he had gotten into the habit of drinking with buddies
down on Front Street every Saturday afternoon. This

particular Saturday night he had accosted a man 30 years his junior (Dad was 63) who was not only younger but a boxer to boot. Struck five times before falling, hitting his head on the curb, dad was DOA at the local hospital. How suddenly life had changed. I could not grasp that Dad was dead, that never again would we go camping up on Mt. Baldy, just he and I, that never again would I put my arm around his neck and say, "Next to God, I love you best."

The echo of rifles barking out a military salute was softened by the winsome sound of Taps as the coffin began slowly descending into the grave, taking with it any hopes I had that this was all a bad dream. It was for real. My hero was gone.

Bad news and good news followed this family tragedy. Life was pretty hollow without Dad. Mother was left a single mom with three children ages 7, 10, and 12, and precious little money to make ends meet, just a small veteran's pension she managed to stretch around expenses. We lost the house a few months after Dad died. Mother sold the car. When we finally left our home on the hill and moved to town, we discovered that country folk don't easily take to apartment living. There were no fields to roam, no irrigation canal to swim in, no more playing with my old friends. The one-room school with eight grades was replaced by a multi-room school with so many students I couldn't begin to learn all their names. It was confusing and depressing.

I scoured every trash can and bin in every alley collecting beer bottles, copper, and aluminum scraps that could be sold to boost the family income. I peddled newspapers on the street corner, sometimes selling only two or three, but even five cents—the big take for the evening—would buy a quart of milk or a loaf of bread. It was the heart of the Great Depression, and we found ourselves gratefully "eating out of the pork barrel," as the locals called the frequent welfare offerings of large oaken barrels of salted pork.

The good news was that mother was a spiritual woman who wanted to have her children grow up with Christian values. Orphaned at the age of two, she was reared in a Roman Catholic orphanage and later a convent. Apparently mother and dad had an understanding that there would be no direct church influence in the home. I can remember only once attending mass and that was on a Christmas Eve. Dad, though a grandson of a Presbyterian minister, made no profession of Christianity.

The very week of the funeral, mother announced that we would start attending church. Which one was optional in her thinking. "We are going to search for a church. We will go to a different one every week until we find one that we like."

Her next announcement caught us totally by surprise: "This week, on Saturday, we are going to visit the Seventh-day Adventist Church." That did not create any excitement, but her next words seemed to promise something a little better to come. "After that we will attend a different one every Sunday until we find the one that seems to fit us best."

So we started out on Saturday morning with a strange feeling that this made no sense at all. It was sort of tipping the hat to some Adventist neighbors who had stopped by every week to share a copy of an Adventist magazine, *Signs of the Times*. As we walked to town, neighbors asked us where we were going all dressed up on Saturday morning. (All dressed up? During the worst of the Depression I suppose you could say that about clean jeans and calico.) We thought it was funny to say we were going to church. After all it was only Saturday morning. Attending church was scary enough as it was. A red face didn't make it easier!

It wasn't as bad as we feared. As it turned out, it was fun: stories and pictures, lots of kids who were friendly, and teachers who made us feel special. "Sabbath School" they called it, and the time went by so fast it almost seemed to be over before it started. Adults we met upstairs were friendly, too. It was a whole new world. But when mother said, "Next week, children, we'll go to another church," we balked as apprehension mounted.

We had "broken the ice" once and didn't want to do it every week. "Why can't we just go back to the Adventist church next week?" we pleaded. And mother relented.

When evangelistic meetings were held in a temporary building in town, we walked the two miles each meeting night, eager to hear the two fiery evangelists sing and preach. A banner over the platform made me think as it fairly shouted, "What shall it profit a man if he gain the whole world and lose his own soul?" It sure caught my attention! It stimulated the first serious religious and philosophic thinking I had ever done. My Catholic mother had taught me to love God and to pray. Now I began to understand why. Now I wanted to become a friend of Jesus and live with Him in heaven. I genuinely surrendered my life to Him, and though I was now only eight years old, I walked out into the Rogue River one Sabbath afternoon and was baptized with a group of other candidates. I have made a lot of foolish decisions through the years, but that decision was one of the best. No regrets, ever. It was the beginning of a forever friendship with Jesus Christ that would someday take me to the ends of earth preaching the Good News to thousands. But I'm getting ahead of the story.

After a couple of years of city living, we moved to a remote area where we lived in a primitive log cabin. No electricity, no running water (unless you call running with a bucket from the spring a quarter of a mile away "running water"), no indoor bathroom, no switches (except the one mother kept for us kids). The logs had large cracks between them. You could practically put the cat out without opening the door! There was plenty of fresh air in the winter even though we had tacked cardboard over the logs on the inside. I tried to beat the freeze at night by placing a warm iron wrapped in newspaper at my feet and pulling the covers up over my face. It was not uncommon to wake up with frost crystals in our hair and ice in the water bucket by the kitchen sink. Deprived? Not really. Poor, sure—so was everybody else. And there were compensations. We lived in a forest of pine and fir trees. There were mountain trails to hike, deer to stalk, a creek to fish, and a summer swimming hole down by the covered bridge a mile or so from home. I often lay on a carpet of pine needles under a tree watching vultures soar endlessly in a Kodachrome sky all the time thinking big thoughts about who I was and what the future held. Deprived? Not on your life. Living in the hills among people some would call hillbillies gave me a down-home perspective on life that has stood me in good stead around the world.

But it was not Eden. I was a member of a religious minority. Wholesome kids from country farms took their time in opening their friendships to kids from "outside." On the first day of school a roughneck came up to me, not even knowing my name, and said, "Hey, kid, how old are you?"

"I'm eleven," I replied.

Quickly he shot back, "I'm only twelve, let's fight." And we did; I got beat up.

Mother, bearing the loss of her husband, rearing three kids who were either teens or nearing that threshold, and doing it on very limited income, had an emotional breakdown. I was failing in school. My fifth-grade teacher and I did not share friendly chemistry. Not realizing that I was within earshot, she told another student I was a failure. I was crushed. I was fast on the way to becoming a case in somebody's psychology book. I was passed on to the sixth grade by profession of faith.

I heard we would have a new teacher in the coming school term, and I was nervous as I trudged up the steps into Evans Valley Union School in September. Change was not always for the better, I feared. As I entered the foyer and turned left down the corridor, I saw her. She was standing at the door greeting each student. "That's a switch," I thought, stepping toward the door.

She reached out, shaking my hand and with a smile asking, "And who are you?"

"I'm Bruce Johnston."

"Oh, I know who you are. I had your older brother and sister in another school. They were wonderful students and I know you will be, too."

Wow, I thought, I not only have problems of my own but now I have the family reputation on my back. At that moment something happened that I can only call a life-changing moment. I had earned enough money during the summer to buy a bright blue shirt with a zipper on the breast pocket. While she spoke, Mrs. Sloan reached out, zipped the zipper open and then shut again. Just that fast. What a small, insignificant gesture. But it struck me like an electrical shock. No, it wasn't static shock! I felt no physical sensation, but it hit me that this woman really liked kids and had reached out to me. She accepted me. Maybe she was right that I would be a good student.

Under the mentoring of this wonderful Christian woman my academic life turned around. My emotional life was touched as well. Low self-image gave way to a brighter outlook. By the end of the school year I was getting the best grades in the class.

Mother struggled and finally could take domestic responsibilities no longer. She asked each of us kids to leave. I was sixteen when my turn came. Brother Bill and his new wife invited me to live with them. Four months later he was drafted into the Navy. I became a foster kid rotating among different church members who braved taking in a teenager. Would anyone question the debt I owe?

The good news at this time was that, though I had attended public schools all my years, I was persuaded to enroll in Rogue River Academy, an Adventist high school.

I didn't particularly want to go there, but I had some friends who insisted that since they had only nine boys to play basketball, they needed someone to round out two intramural teams!

After only a few days of running into more rules than I thought existed, though, I decided to drop out and attend the local public high school. My Scottish blood kept reminding me that I had paid hard-earned money down; I should have some of it coming back. The principal, Mr. Kenneth Groves, later to become Assistant Business Manager at Walla Walla College, didn't refuse or scold. That took me by surprise. It was the first time I had been treated man to man. He explained, "You have been here just a few days. I know it has been a difficult transition from high school to the academy. But we need you here and we think you need us. Why don't you give it two weeks—then if you still want to go, come in. I'll refund your entrance fee and there will be no questions asked." It was fair enough for me. I stayed two years.

Graduating, I had no plan for the future. I had made my way by working at a service station owned by a man named Babcock, picking fruit in an orchard, and driving truck. A friend and I built a makeshift trailer house, and we batched the summer after graduation.

Enter another life-changing event. At camp meeting in Gladstone Park, Oregon, I ran into Lee Roy Holmes, a friend who had enrolled in the summer session at Walla Walla College. (Lee Roy later became an educator and pastor. He said that I had a big influence on his life, that when we were juniors at Rogue River Academy I had asked a group of my classmates standing around the wood-burning stove one morning before classes began, "What are you going to do with your life?" He says that got him thinking seriously about his future. I confess that I cannot remember having a thought that profound at that particular time, but I do remember the tremendous influence he had on me.) He was excited, a condition I thought somewhat bizarre, especially when he explained that he was taking Greek and studying for the ministry. "Bruce," he implored, "you've got to come to college." Oh, sure, I thought. It's O.K. for you living in the village with your parents, but how can a homeless guy without financial support ever make it in college? I was to find out. A seed had been sown.

A recruiter from Walla Walla College came in mid-summer to visit my friend. Why he didn't have my name I did not discover, but when he found that I'd just finished high school, he zeroed in. Thanks, but no thanks, I thought. I had no plan for it and no intention. But one thing in my short life I had learned and it was to be reinforced: things change, often rapidly.

September came. College had already started. An alien thought intruded: "Bruce, what are you going to do with your life?" I had no answer. It struck me that college might have the answer, and there was no time to lose. I put my car up for sale, and it sold quickly. I now had money to get started, with perhaps enough left over to take me a couple of quarters down the track if I got the job promised by the recruiter. I told my trailer-house friend my plans, that I was leaving on the approaching Sunday to hitchhike to Walla Walla. Clair, who was a college dropout with no interest at the moment, said, "You'll have to go through Portland. I'll hitchhike with you that far and get a job."

At 7:00 Sunday morning we stood at the outskirts of Medford, Oregon, on Highway 99 at the big Y made by its junction with the Crater Lake Highway. Two hours later, Clair threw in the towel. "We're never going to get a ride. I'm going to go over to the Big Y Market and get a job." He did and worked there two years. By 5:30 p.m. I was not only terribly hungry, but I was also only 30 miles away in Grants Pass, a mere 520 miles short of Walla Walla! Being of a quick turn of mind, it dawned that I was not going to get to Walla Walla College that day. Spending the night along the highway was a prospect to avoid. I walked across the road and stuck out my thumb. The first car that came by whisked me right back to Medford, where I had started more than ten hours before. Ten hours one way, 30 minutes the other! The mathematics seemed to suggest that college was not in my future; otherwise, God would have seen to it that I got better rides.

Mr. Babcock looked up from pumping gas, surprised. (It was at his service station that I used to hang out and work on my car. Sometimes I pumped gas and did light mechanical work for him.) "Hey, you're supposed to be at Walla Walla College. What are you doing here?"

"Well, I tried all day but I didn't make it. I guess God doesn't want me to go."

"Oh, yes, He does," was his reply, "and tomorrow I'm going to take you." He hired someone to pump gas and by mid-afternoon the next day I'd been deposited on the campus of Walla Walla College, while Mr. Babcock headed home, a round trip of over 1,000 miles. The phenomenal thing, as I look back, is that this man, who had little formal education, saw something in me to encourage toward more education. It was one of those significant hinges in time where a little nudge changed the course of another person's life. As a result, I was now on my way to a future brighter than anything I ever dreamed of in early years, lying on a cushion of pine needles, watching the vultures soar and thinking big thoughts.

A lesson I learned early in life is that we not only do things with each other but we do things to each other. Later, when I became a pastor, I took a morning walk. Crossing the Mellon Street bridge, I paused to watch a lazy current drift beneath the bridge. On an impulse, I threw a pebble into the lake-like surface. There was a splash and then a rippled circle appeared. Then another, and another, until the circles reached each bank and above and under the bridge. It was only a tiny pebble.

How much like that life is. We scarcely think how significant is a little act of kindness or generosity. We

11

sometimes think our lives don't make much difference. Who would be the worse for it if we just dropped out? Whose reward will it be for preaching to thousands and seeing multitudes come to Christ? Who can say but that in the celestial bookkeeping Mr. Babcock's share will be equal or more?

It is beyond the scope of this writing to relate the "rest of the story." But I was now on my way to a satisfying and exciting life that would include being a pastor, a college teacher, a missionary training pastors and conducting public Gospel meetings, a mission pilot flying mercy missions over the jungles of Borneo, a church administrator, and even the Chairman of the Board of Walla Walla College! That's a long way for a hillbilly boy who failed fifth grade.

I walked through the Gateway to Service upon graduation from Walla Walla College seriously recognizing the debt I owed to so many and not the least to Walla Walla College. (It was not financial. Without any family help I had made it through, and when I walked across the stage in Columbia Auditorium and was handed my diploma folder, the college owed me seventeen dollars!) I had all the help I needed from God, who arranged more work opportunities than I could handle, and all the encouragement from people whom He had impressed to give me nudges at those appropriate moments when I needed them most.

Bruce Johnston is a 1949 theology graduate of Walla Walla College. He served as chair of the WWC board from 1986-1996, while he was president of the North Pacific Union Conference of Seventh-day Adventists.

Psalm Under a Green Cathedral

Willful spirit
I
Am humbled
restrained
By who You are

What, who am I
That You are mindful of me?
That You would plant me breathless
Under a skyline of unabashed color
That You would let me taste the wonder of creation
In the form of two small boys
That you would let me go my own way
While hoping I would choose yours.

Stopped in my tracks
I bow
Under this green cathedral
awed, again
By this life-full, green revelation of You

I come full and hungry

Brimming over
My soul
Spills its adoration on You

All the while hungry,
longing for You to create in me
Stillness of soul
Attentiveness of heart
Willingness, in place of willfulness

Make my life
Rooted
Like the umbrella of summer green locusts and maples
Able to create shade and nourishment
For others
Even as you have done
For me.

Amen.

Written on College Avenue, in front of the Ad building, in summer shade.

—*Delona Bell*

Delona Lang Bell, a 1979 graduate of Walla Walla College, writes from Walla Walla where she and her husband, Michael (WWC 1980), and their two sons live.

An Ivy League School

Susan Bungard

I didn't believe in love at first sight until I walked into my first college classroom. It wasn't planned. It wasn't anticipated. It just happened. I looked at those 25 students and was enraptured with the idea of knowing each one of them and sharing myself as well as my passion for writing with them. Many, many classes later, I know that teaching is not about a job; it's about love. Not only that, but it's about love that can transform the world, student by student, person by person.

Admittedly, I'm not this gushy at midnight with a pile of essays in front of me. I'm not gleeful at 6 a.m. when preparing for classes. Teaching is endlessly hard work because it never seems finished. It never is finished. Yet when I walk into a classroom each day, I am renewed with the realization that students sit before me for only brief moments in the span of their lives, and it is an incredible opportunity to share those moments together in a meaningful way. Of course, I also urge the importance of clear, effective, innovative writing; curious, critical reading, and proper grammar and punctuation. Some of this, my students will, I hope, remember. Even more, though, I hope they will remember that the classroom they sat in at that point in their lives was filled with love—unapologetic and infectious love. Now that is memorable!

Cultivating love in a classroom isn't like turning on a light or pushing a power button. It takes time and patience, like any relationship. Some students bloom and flourish easily. Some seem indifferent and distant at first; others discouraged and lost. It is impossible to reach all at the same time. It is possible to reach all—whether the listless, the bored, the amused, the bemused, the enthused—only in time, but not my time. God's time. Love can take root and grow in unforeseen, transforming ways from a classroom into life, into relationships, into the future.

My confidence in classroom cultivation is certainly not based on any sort of horticultural prowess; in fact, I have a horrible history with houseplants. Whether to a hearty, industrial potted plant, or a fragile bouquet of fresh flowers, I'm an unwitting assassin. I may water and sun and trim and prod and coax and whine, but they all, prematurely, die. This was true, that is, until Valentine's Day, 1998. I was sent a dozen beautiful, healthy, and I imagined, doomed roses. But with Cupid's nudging, I made it my mission to keep those roses alive. Every day I tended and gazed and willed those flowers to thrive. I watched the petals gracefully spread open, the delicate shades of red change, and wondered at the exquisite beauty of each fragrant flower in the bouquet. To my amazement, the roses lived and lived, even outlasting the relationship whence they had come! So was it that particular cut of roses? Was it the soil in which they had grown? Or was it the loving attention and admiration they were given? The love, I say—it was the love!

Are students, are people, any different from those roses? No—students need care and attention and nurturing, too. I haven't met a student yet who wouldn't, in some form, accept compassion when it was individualized to him or her. It may not be well-traveled, but there is a path to each person's heart. And when that heart is touched, even in the slightest but most loving way, it changes a person. Maybe not at that moment, maybe not even perceptibly soon, but someday it will. That is the transforming quality of love—the love that comes from God.

Of course, touching other people's lives isn't confined to the classroom. That's what is so exciting about it—it can happen anywhere and grow everywhere! Consider ivy on old buildings like the Walla Walla College Administration building. It sprawls; it crawls; it climbs shamelessly up the bricks, into crevices; around windows and corners ivy reaches, it embraces. That's what love can do with small, significant kindnesses shown to each other—not just in the classroom but—everywhere. Somewhere, though, it has to start.

It might begin with smiling. It's simple. It's bright. It's life-giving. Once it gets to be a habit, it becomes a natural and beautiful facial feature.

Then there's eye contact. Also simple. Giving eye attention is a sign of giving heart attention. It decreases misunderstanding and increases bonding.

A more challenging act of kindness is listening. Truly listening involves not fidgeting or interrupting, and paying attention to what the person is saying rather than what we are expecting or wanting to hear.

More challenging still is the ability to be vulnerable and honest. People know when they are connecting with real people, and when they don't, both go away empty. Yet vulnerability has the potential of emptying one person while filling the other and then returning even more fully to the first.

Another important principle is looking for the good in other people. It is always refreshing to find interesting, fun, unique, and somehow endearing qualities about other people. It might take a scavenger hunt, but tireless searching will bring a prize. Everyone has prizes.

Practicing small but significant deeds of kindness for other people also makes a difference. These may involve a bit of time, but not more than it takes to drink a cup of tea or catch up on the news. Kindnesses involve genuine notes of appreciation, compliments, or encouragement; or cookies or flowers or balloons. Kindnesses include stopping to talk for more than a moment, or giving a hug, or sharing a prayer. The effect of these gestures? It grows and grows inside and then outside of the person who was touched.

Not everyone can do all these things all the time. Trying to fulfill them isn't the idea; letting them become part of a lifestyle is. There could be veritable collisions of kindnesses all around! A world transformed.

That's what I see when I look at a college classroom— a small world of students to love as well as teach who, in turn, will grow and love. It's not about a job; it's about ivy.

Susan Bungard is a 1981 graduate of Walla Walla College. She has taught English composition at Walla Walla College since 1990.

Entering the Sabbath

Todd Schoepflin

I shift to a more comfortable position on the lab stool in the electronics lab and glance at my watch. Almost 5:00. I quickly modify the code and recompile my program, but the bug remains. Instead of trying again, I turn off the computer, pick up my briefcase, and enter the Sabbath as I hear the door close behind me. The light of the setting sun creates a gradient of grays and blues as I head west across Bade Street to Heubach Chapel.

As usual, there are only two or three of us. We turn uncomfortably in the pews to chat. A few more straggle in. After a pause, someone suggests we start. Our group clasps hands in the aisle, forming an oval. One by one, we raise each other and our campus to God. Burdens and triumphs mingle as we speak. When the last person finishes, we squeeze hands and wander out of the chapel.

However, my religion professor, Alden Thompson, and I have not yet finished entering the Sabbath. We walk past the main entry of the College church and take the side entrance. Mike and Keith have already dimmed the lights and lit the candles in the youth room. We join them on the floor and Mike flips on the portable stereo. Traditional Jewish music flows forth as we watch the flickering candles.

After several minutes, Keith passes out the responsive reading translated from Jewish liturgy. I fancy myself nearer to the ancients as we recount how God has blessed God's people. One particular sentence still strikes me:

"We have not kept the Sabbath. The Sabbath has kept us."

Next, we sing a few songs with the tape, using the words Mike has typed and photocopied. The songs are often pitched too high and the words are strange. Nevertheless, we sing the now familiar "Diminu" as the candles drip messily. Quiet settles in on us. We pray briefly and then partake of some grape juice. But the moment cannot last forever. Someone turns the overhead fluorescent lights back on, and we say goodbye as we separate to celebrate the Sabbath elsewhere.

Todd Schoepflin is a 1997 electrical engineering graduate of Walla Walla College. He is a doctoral student in electrical engineering at the University of Washington.

Stuffed Teddy Bears

Sandy Zaugg

My two-year-old granddaughter is totally occupied with arranging her stuffed bears in a pattern seen only with her own eyes. She glances up occasionally to be certain I'm still there. She smiles, giggles, and gets back to her work.

I love her so much. I want the best for her. I want her to succeed in life. I want her to add goodness to the world, to make a difference. But right now, she can only arrange stuffed bears—and giggle.

Does the Lord look at me in the same way? Loving me so much, wanting me to add His goodness to the world, watching over me while I do my insignificant busy work? Is He fondly, patiently waiting for me to grow up?

Sandy Zaugg is a 1961 graduate of Walla Walla College. Since 1988 she has served as an associate dean of women and an English as a second language teacher at Walla Walla College.

Sinai and Salvation: Reflections on a Pilgrimage

Jim Robertson

It was 2:30 a.m. The red granite gravel crunched beneath our feet in the darkness. The few flashlights in the group searched out the path ahead. We could sense on our right the massive walls of St. Catherine's monastery at the base of Mount Sinai, but the blackness of the desert night swallowed any sense of sight.

"Slow down, slow down! You'll wear yourselves out before you get there," Sharon called from the back of the line. "There" was the top of Mount Sinai, where we were headed to watch the sunrise. But her warning went unheeded and soon the line of 20 people had sorted itself into five groups moving at different paces. Before long the gaps between us grew until we could no longer hear conversations of those ahead or behind.

Towering above us in the darkness, faintly outlined against the spangled desert sky, was the mountain where Moses met God and talked with Him. We were ascending in the footsteps of innumerable pilgrims before us. Perhaps we, like they, hoped to experience for ourselves a sense of God's lingering presence on the mountain.

Our tour leader left us directions but was unable to accompany us. "You can't get lost," he said. "There's only one trail and it will be obvious." But shortly after leaving the monastery, we had trouble finding the obvious. The rocks and sand off the trail looked about the same as the trail. Several times we fanned out, calling to each other until someone said, "Oh, here it is!"

Once the trail started climbing more steeply, the way became clear.

Looking up at the massive darkness of Sinai, I was amazed at how many flashlights blinked and bobbed along the trail to the top. Those people must have left long before midnight to be that far up the mountain.

After 45 minutes of steady climbing, we came upon one of our groups that had been moving faster. They had stopped to repair Dave's sandal. The strap that went beside the big toe had pulled through the sole. The eight of us aimed flashlights at the broken footwear and suggested ways of repairing it. We rummaged through fanny packs and pockets for bits of wire or string or whatever else might work and managed a temporary fix. We shared some hard candy and water and consolation with Dave. Then it was back to the darkness, trudging at a measured pace up the hill, not sure what lay around the next switchback or rock outcrop.

Coming around a bend in the trail, we were surprised to find civilization: a kerosene lantern threw its yellow light against the night, and a Bedouin emerged from a hut, offering chocolate, coffee, Pepsi, souvenirs and even a camel to take us to the top if our legs were giving out. We passed by without stopping.

Several times other groups, dark faceless shapes with light at their feet, passed us, or we would pass them. We exchanged greetings in English, and they resumed their German or French once they passed. Looking back down the mountain into the darkness from which we had ascended, we saw more lights following our own.

The trail grew steeper. We were walking next to vertical granite walls on our left when we came to a fork in the trail. Following our directions, we turned left and saw the trail abruptly change from sandy gravel to stone steps that had been carved into the solid granite centuries ago by monks from St. Catherine's. The darkness that clung to us permitted no visual reference, but we knew from our breathing and perspiration that we were climbing steeply.

Dawn had not yet cracked the eastern horizon when we arrived at the top of Mt. Sinai. More surprises awaited. Immediately in front of us was a small stone church. The bell on the small steeple stood out against the tiny sliver of moon. We stepped over people in sleeping bags who had spent the night huddled next to its walls. Coming around the end of the church we found another Bedouin shop. This tent was almost a department store, with several lanterns illuminating its extensive wares. Some pilgrims browsed there, impatient for dawn.

More amazing to me was the number of people— probably 200—on top of Mount Sinai at 5 a.m. Some stood in small groups sipping hot, sweet Arab tea; others crouched together to keep warm. Quiet laughter and conversation in many languages rose and fell.

Our little group found more of our party and sat on a large, sloping slab of granite to watch for the sunrise and wait for other members of our group to arrive. We hadn't been cold during the exertion of the climb, but now, sitting in our sweat-soaked clothes, we shivered. Gradually the sky in the east grew light. The camera shutter clunked slowly as I recorded the growing orange glow. A group of French pilgrims sang religious songs. It reminded me of music I'd heard in films when French young people sang as they made their way along the country roads to Chartres Cathedral in the spring.

The last of our group arrived just as the sun emerged over the desert landscape. It included Dave, who had given up on his broken sandal and made the trip barefoot. Also in that group were George, slowed by bad knees, and his mother, Cleoma, who was about to turn 64.

The rising sun brought color to the world of gray. The tortured granite folds of Mount Sinai and its neighboring peaks turned rusty rose. The warming light brought colors to clothes and skin, shape to faces and beards, and made the once mysterious pilgrim shapes look much more like ourselves.

In the full light of morning I gazed over the 360-degree view. Ridge after ridge of mountains and wadis marched to the horizon. If this was the mountain Moses had been on, he certainly had quite a view for 40 days. Was this the very spot where God had come down to the earth and given His law? Was it in this immense stillness that God's voice spoke directly to Moses? I sat in silence letting the possibility that it might be soak into my soul. I picked up a small piece of red granite and put it in my pocket to share with others who would never have the opportunity to be here.

Soon it was time to start back down the mountain before the day grew too hot. Letting gravity help me down the stairs, I marveled at how different it all looked in the light. How the stairs were cut into the rock made sense to me. The path, with all its twists and turns, seemed so plain now. Whoever had made the trail had obviously followed the easiest route through the difficult terrain. How could we, only hours before, have been confused or have doubted which way it went?

As the granite steps gave way to the sloping, sandy trail, I pondered how much the experience of salvation might parallel that climb up Mount Sinai.

The people in our group all started out together with the same goal in mind. But we were not the only group climbing the mountain of God. Many had gone before us, not just that dark morning, but for thousands of years before. Our group with its diverse personalities split up into smaller ones that travelled at different paces.

Unexpected events slowed some down. None of us had ever been where we were going, so it was unfamiliar territory. We may have had some preconceived ideas of what it might be like, but the actual experience was different. We did, however, trust the directions we were given because our tour leader had made the trip before us.

Each person brought a different level of physical fitness to the task. For some it was a much more difficult climb than for others. Each person experienced that climb in his or her own way. Along the journey, there was a lot of sharing of candy, water, and conversation. During the dark hours we got to know each other at a far deeper and more signficant level than we had while riding in comfort on the tour bus. Walking next to someone in the dark, it was easy to talk of the real issues in our lives—our hopes and dreams, our disappointments and pains. We slowed or stopped when someone in our group needed to, and we stopped as a group to offer help to others. As fellow pilgrims and travelers, we experienced a definite sense of "we're all in this together."

There was no shortcut to the top. The only way we could get there was to put one foot in front of the other and keep going, taking comfort that the lights bobbing on the mountain high above meant that what we were attempting was possible. Faith told us the process would produce the desired destination, but the length of time for each group or person to reach the top varied, as did the degree of difficulty or ease for each individual.

Some people had better flashlights than others. Some people had no flashlights at all but were able to complete the trip by staying close to those who did. Each one walked in the light that was available.

When we reached the top of the mountain and realized we were where God's presence had been literally and visibly manifested, we were glad. The bus trip through the desert, the 1:30 a.m. rising, the long and arduous uphill walk through the dark hours, seemed well worth it. Such words of encouragement and congratulations we shared with each other! Such joy to find all the members of our group once we had reached the top! Not one was missing!

Besides our group of 20, we found many more people

up there than we could have imagined: people of different languages, nationalities and theological belief systems. Each had followed the light available and now stood in the fulness of daylight on the mountain of God. The sun was shining in its full strength, making plain everything that had been obscure or puzzling during the long climb in the dark.

Words of Scripture came to mind: "But you are a chosen race, a royal priesthood, a holy nation, God's own people, in order that you may proclaim the mighty acts of him who called you out of darkness into his marvelous light" 1 Peter 2:9 NRSV.

Jim Robertson is a 1969 theology graduate of Walla Walla College. He teaches religion at Portland Adventist Academy.

Working My Way

Harold Lamberton

The value of things such as gold or diamonds or degrees such as Ph.D. or M.D. seems to be directly related to how hard one has to work to find the things or be awarded the degrees.

At the end of the Great Depression most of my classmates at Walla Walla College had to struggle to have enough income from campus jobs to stay in school. When a new quarter began, we had to obtain a permit to attend classes from Mr. Peterson at the business office. (This permit was a card somewhat like a credit card of today only made on cardboard since plastic was not yet in use).

My Adventist education was an answer to many emotional prayers leveled at God by me and my Mamma and Papa Lamberton. I was number eight in a family of 14 children. There was no extra money for attending Yakima Valley Academy or Walla Walla College. The entrance fee at Walla Walla College in those days was thirty-five dollars. I learned that by feverishly picking apples at three cents a box, I could earn the thirty-five dollars over and above what I contributed to help support our large family. Then I had to face what to do for money after the first financial period ended and the time came to obtain the next card from the College business office.

Not just my family and I struggled but so did everyone else. What made it possible for us to stay in school were the college industries. All Seventh-day Adventist colleges in those days had industries that employed students. At Walla Walla College the college farm, dairy, print shop, book bindery, college store, laundry, auto mechanics shop, body and fender shop, and Walla Walla General Hospital provided jobs for students.

At my entrance interview, Mr. Peterson discovered that I was a farm boy and that I knew how to milk cows. He rubbed his hands together and said, "Good, we need more milkers" (there were no milk machines in those days). So every morning at 4:30 a.m. and after my last class every afternoon at 4:30 p.m., I would rush down to my room in an old house dubbed "Banker's Mansion," get into old clothes, and run out to the barn and milk. The pay was eight cents a cow. Those big old Holstein milk cows had huge udders, and it was hard to get the milk pail between their teats and the floor. Each cow usually gave three gallons each milking. With eight cows in my string I made $ .64 every morning and $ .64 every evening. That daily total of $1.28 paid for my room and most of my food. I got extra jobs doing janitor work in the administration building classrooms. I was paid a certain amount per month for each room. I could dust erasers and wash the blackboards twice as fast as the elderly man who was paid by the hour to clean some of the rooms.

One of my sisters (Helen) and a brother (Forest) went all the way back to Madison College in Tennessee, where they worked for seven cents an hour. Helen worked her way through nurse's training. She worked through all holiday vacations and the summer vacations. She stayed the entire four years without once coming home.

Cooperation of the church, the college, and the student made it possible to get through college. I doubt that it would be possible today. I, Harold Lamberton, my siblings, and my parents have been forever thankful for being provided these opportunities to get through school.

Harold Lamberton, MD, is a 1942 graduate of Walla Walla College. He is retired and lives in Walla Walla, Washington.

Yosemite Chapel

Nate Williams

I walked in, trying to be as quiet as God and hoped no one would be there except God. As I pushed the glass-framed doors open they made no noise that I can remember, but if they did, it was lost in a kind of Holy hum, echoing against itself, pulling me in, and shutting the doors. It was like a daydream, a room of dusty light—it was as if someone's fingers were plugging my ears and I was listening to a waterfall, somewhere far away, continually crumble from its head to its feet. Two short rows of wooden pews knelt toward the front, a cross hung on the wall, and below it a table, like a stocky pillar, supported two white candles in gold stands that guarded an open Bible. I found the Book turned to Acts, chapter twelve. It was about Peter, and the Lord rescuing him from prison. I wondered if it was supposed to mean something special, like some divine hand had turned it to that page for me. Whatever it was, I felt like this Presence must be the only thing that could give me answers and peace of mind; I felt it like a large apple might feel a little seed deep within its core.

I played my whistle, the way I always did when I was alone in a church, letting prayers in my head flow through my breath and fingers and entwine themselves with the unbroken calm of the chapel. Then I left like the notes did, gone but still there under the surface of silence. I'm still there now, playing my whistle in the quiet, and waiting.

I found more than my own presence in that chapel,

and I played for more than just myself. A Pulse I'd never felt before filled my being with itself, yet I didn't know how to touch it, didn't know how to speak to it, didn't know how to be in it. I wanted more out of spiritual existence than just hanging around, and not knowing why, and pretending to be content. I wanted to go beyond, but I didn't know where to start, how to ask, or believe.

When I was ten years old my church youth club would go into neighborhoods on the coldest and rainiest nights and collect canned goods. I would say "please" and "thank-you" and never walk on their lawn when they were looking. I learned my memory verses and read the back of the church's children's magazine; I even made cheese sandwiches and bought underwear from Fred Meyer and helped give them to the homeless. I grew up always believing, but when I started taking God and spirituality seriously, it stopped. Like a trained parrot, I squawked out the faith of my parents and church, never truly questioning what I mimicked, never truly searching out, for myself, what I believed and why. I always had the capability and freedom to do this, but never realized the incredible need until now. So I became a sort of atheist, starting from the bottom, but still hoping and searching. That Yosemite chapel became a physical place where all the nothingness, all the blindness could come together.

Churches—temples—holy places—all seem to hold a power of peace and tranquility that everyone, at sometime, experiences. I met this girl last summer who always had a little sticker in the middle of her forehead; she had a nose ring too, and a laugh that sounded like wind blowing over a brook. She would sit cross-legged, pull a cigarette out, tuck her dyed hair behind her ears, and shyly puff away behind a mischievous smile. She loved to go to mosques—she told me the priests there were so kind—accepting—and when she sat there, alone, she felt whole. Going to such places to be silent is common. But what's more common is the going to the market for food. I wonder how silence and holiness puzzle together with the sustaining of life.

All over the world people have attempted to house their gods—to create a place where they can come to their god. Whatever the god, wherever the house, there is at sometime a quietness; and in that quietness humanity finds something beyond itself—a divine presence—which they know they need, but don't always admit to.

If I never bathed I would smell utterly foul—and over time not even know it—but were I ever to bathe I would realize how much I really needed it, how good it made me feel and smell; and then I could never live without bathing again. The Divine Presence is the awakening—a realization—a warm rain you can never do without again.

All humanity, whether they realize it or not, is searching for God. I only wish that faith could be more addictive—affect your soul and body—give you a spiritual warmth that would guide your mind and body toward God's will. Maybe, though, it's better the way it is—a trust deep within you that can't be misplaced, and nobody can take away.

Nate Williams is an English major at Walla Walla College.

Autumn Quarter

Happy are those
    who do not follow
    the advice of the wicked,

or take the path that sinners tread,
    or sit in the seat of scoffers;

but their delight is
    in the law of the Lord,
    and on his law
    they meditate day and night.

They are like trees
    planted by streams of water,

which yield their fruit in its season,
    and their leaves do not wither.

In all that they do, they prosper.

                Psalm 1:13, NRSV

Rationality is an Inferior Form of Discourse

Leanne Veverka

This is not an argument. Not in the classical sense. The eternal triangle takes a breather. The whole is greater than the sum of the parts. A Hellenic temple, complete in itself amidst the starry unknown. The water cycle chasing its tail through time, not realizing the tail is the mouth. Like an octave writ large. For the sum of the parts may be a sunny day or π or Tycho Brahe, but Tycho and I can sit down for a bite of π and wash it down with a sunny day and not mind at all. This is nonsense. Of course, this is not an argument.

a   young girl slips on her mothers wedding gown
and peers shyly into the mirror   beethoven
          composes
          his ninth symphony one lone hawk hangs
motionless
     and golden above the trees below
the   peaks in the center of the world i survey
as i look

                              down from
my lofty perch to   peek over her shoulder she
turns and looks the platonic solids

                              nestled
     each by each in keplers mind as the planets whirl in
their elliptical

                              orbits crickets myzithra
cheese   and not getting sick during summer

vacation the cafe in prague where they
spoke english and served the best pesto in
the world a wee

blond lad
pipes there are gocs in the irsh
where a now grown girl once threw herself in
with the

bread wipe that grin
off your face mona im trying to
paint here and the
little goatfooted balloonman whistles   far
and wee do you
recall what was
the feel

the day the music
died

moliere tweaks the
noses of the nobles and   they love him for it a
very tired girl drags to her feet to give a
nun her
seat on the train the smell of lilacs at dusk
the remembered sound of horns

The unanswered question often has more power, more
meaning, than the neatly packaged, gel-coated, easy to
swallow, sanitized for your pleasure, there-is-a-right-
answer-and-it's-mine type of question. Imagine a couple.
The man asks the woman, "Do you love me?" She doesn't
answer. Meaning? Yes. But what is it? Who knows . . . .
Three million things could be running through her head,
keeping her from answering yea or nay. Maybe she
doesn't love him. Maybe she responded in some
nonverbal way. But the question hangs there. The man
will not be satisfied until he gets an answer. He will ask
more questions. Or wish he had. Otherwise, he'll never
know who she is. Even by asking questions, he'll reach
only an approximation. And every approximation is an

abstraction. And every abstraction is random. Why am I a female vs. a Caucasian vs. an American vs. an intellectual vs. a cat lover vs. a brunette vs. a potential car buyer vs. a Tolkien enthusiast? If I can only be described abstractly, randomly, how can I describe a Supreme Being with any more accuracy?

                              tell me a story daddy is
        poetry the form or the intent or the intensity feminism
is the radical notion that   women are people two
            plus two equals four elderly people offering
                                        extra ketchup
                    packets from their purses and
smiling toothlessly hurt not the earth people
                  in glass
        houses should invest in robes the professor
  pulls a   book from the shelf and
with the dust falls a sprig of mint dry but drenched in
images flowing
out with its cool pale scent the great hulking man
      pulls into the gravel on the side of the road and parks
his bike fixes the floral ladies flat
      tire and hands

                                        her a tract of
                        john and a smile purring piles
                        of closed eyed kittens the
midnight gong of the
        whitman clock the christmas tree ten minutes before it
has to
        come down guavas tree frogs duct   tape

Truth is a logical fallacy. Logic is a system for determining internal consistency. It can guarantee validity correct procedure but not truth. Yet philosophy aspires to reach for truth; building from unverifiable premises, it reaches for the eternal. Which philosophy can never reach, because it cannot prove anything beyond its relationships.

So the philosopher is not so different from the theist. Both try to conceive what is beyond their conception. And they mount the donkey Paradox and ride it to kingdom come, yelling their debates from opposite ends of the saddle. Saddle, sadder, saddest. Debate is by nature divisive. It requires participants to take up opposing viewpoints. No opposition = no debate. Last time I looked, the world came in every color imaginable and some that are better left to the imagination. How realistic is black/white? Has anyone else ever noticed that most debates end unfinished? They reach no across-the-board conclusions. The strongest argument has holes. The mutual hole highlighting of debate lends itself to stasis. To indecision. To holism. And only then to truth.

                    when everything goes
wrong except right when the cycle of life is broken and a
            mother cries why the time a spider bit
                        me and my arm played
balloon games and three in the morning
                saw me in the emergency room and
didnt even   acknowledge me
and
i had to
                get an iv but im terrified of
      needles and i
             almost fainted but my dad held
my hand
      there was one more round trip left
     in the tank konrad lorenz playing mother duck birth
            is the beginning of death the
antelopes eat the
 grass the lions eat the antelopes the lions
   die
   decompose and
   feed the grass sunrise in the blues we hold these truths
to be

                              self evident and the little lady
        presses her nose to the cantaloupes in the supermarket
                        then

                                buys strawberries instead
        why
            is the sky blue daddy every silver lining has a cloud
                            every vegas
                        showgirl has a heart of gold and i have
                                                    feet of clay

To see the whole we must stand at the center. To stand
outside is to have an obstructed view, to see less than the
whole, to lose a sense of the whole. We must relinquish
our distance and let the experiences gang up on us, flow
around us, and remind us that we, too, are part of the
whole. Our stories touch other stories. Our endings are
others' beginnings. And we aren't reading the story; we
are the characters. But the author is not in the story. First
cause, master designer, that than which nothing greater can
be conceived, essence of causality, essence of moral
causality, the great author. Each argument adds a piece.
Each random image adds a piece. A piece to a sum to a
greater whole. To pick the whole to pieces destroys it.
Unravel a tapestry, and all that's left is a pile of string.

    the day he looks at her wrinkled and asleep and knows
                            she said i love you all along a
        teenager
                            stalks defiant into the room and
        crumbles she
                    dumped me standing in the circle of
            light in the pantheon stalking   dreams across
        a moonlit meadow hearing the music of the spheres in
                            dufays motet for the dedication of the
            dome   of the florence   cathedral the
                        london underground at rush
        hour too garlicky spaghetti sauce that i

                                                    ate
                        because
he made   it for me and no
                other reason on earth would
    have
        persuaded me where
                                        does music go two
dogs walking   their people meet and greet on the
grassy lawn of
                the park a childs first   steps first
construction
    paper valentine made with far too
        much elmers glue   and far too little
                        manual dexterity first kiss first
heartbreak the   distinction of being
        owned by the only clumsy cat known to
        humankind the old men   trying so
                    hard to remember
    to say humankind instead of man   my ancient
                            grandmother and her yoda
                hair happening
                        across a patch of
        violets
            in a brown spring

Order in chaos. Chaos in order. Infinity travels in all
directions, out and in. The philosophical scales balance as
the debate blows holes in everyone's boat, and as we sink
into dark waters where do we turn? Our lives flash before
our eyes. Memories. Experiences. Our stories. Our view
of the whole. In the postmodern world of chaotic order
and orderly chaos, pre-formed fish sticks of logic are too
distant, too unreal. What touches, what moves, what
affects: there lies action, decision. Game, set, and match.
A new form of logic arises, the logic of the story, the logic
of connections and relationships. A living logic. Not a
code, a system, a prescription. More like a being? A

wholeness.

        the expression on the teachers face when he reads
the strangest   paper a student has ever written
the freedom
    the student feels
    in saying there is

                        more to
        this than rules   and forms a
                    little boy walks up to the
minister and asks   where is my daddy and
    the minister realizes the boy   is his nephew the
narrow miss

                that moment on space mountain when the
track goes   whoosh down and then   whoosh to
    the right very quickly and someone is
                                bound to lose a hand
                    but no one ever does a horde of ducklings
                following a female
duck
    across a
        busy   road and life stands still
        for a moment
deciding that life isn't worth it anymore
    then remembering   why it is fresh tomatoes
plucked from a backyard   garden laughing
                    until we cry crying until we laugh
waking up at dawn   and seeing venus
                    hanging low on the
horizon in a bed of orangemelon
                                lemonfruitpunch glow

Of course, this is not an argument. This is nonsense. For
the sum of the parts may be a sunny day or π or Tycho
Brahe, but Tycho and I can sit down for a bite of π and
wash it down with a sunny day and not mind at all. Like
an octave writ large. The water cycle chasing its tail

through time, not realizing the tail is the mouth. A Hellenic temple, complete in itself amidst the starry unknown. The whole is greater than the sum of the parts. The eternal triangle takes a breather. Not in the classical sense. This is not an argument.

Leanne Veverka is a 1999 humanites graduate of Walla Walla College.

I'm 50

The looking forwards-to are past:
high school graduation, college graduation,
wedding, graduate school, babies.
I snatch contentment
from the edges of meeting with students,
grading papers, setting up science labs,
preparing statistics lectures,
grocery shopping, vacuuming.
Life is this moment.

The mirror teaches me how aging looks.
I've seen Santa Claus, yet never knew that eyebrows go
grey,
I wonder if eyelashes do.
A few more creases about the mouth,
a tiredness in the eyes,
Twenty additional pounds under the big shirts and
sweaters,
one spidery magenta line on the top of my left leg,

I'm 50.
Why does that sound so old?
I know that I am perhaps looking forward to fewer years
than I look back to. I notice pedestrians who are older than
me—
all the while counting those younger who outnumber
        the older ones.

I'm 50.
Incongruity settles on my girlish heart in an aging body,
hoping to be the center of attention—content to watch.

I'm 50.
Finally, the pain of my students awakens me.
We pray together.
I listen to baby worries,
hopes for a job,
flashbacks of an abusive childhood,
remorse over love's disappointment.

I'm fifty.
Why did it take so long?

—*Gail Rittenbach*

Gail Rittenbach is a professor of education and psychology at Walla Walla College, where she has taught since 1986.

I Serve a Living and Loving God

Sam Sih

"He will feed His flock like a shepherd; He will gather the lambs with His arm, and carry them in His bosom, and gently lead those who are with young" (Isaiah 40:11, NKJV).

"Thus says the Lord, your Redeemer, the Holy One of Israel. 'I am the Lord your God, who teaches you to profit, who leads you by the way you should go'" (Isaiah 48:17, NKJV).

I was born in China. My father was a successful merchant. My parents joined a nearby Seventh-day Adventist church in Shanghai when I was about seven years old. They brought me to the church for worship, and I attended the children's class. Later on, I studied the correspondence school lessons of the church, and I finished the whole set of correspondence school lessons. I read the Bible often.

When the Chinese Communists came into power in mainland China, the society changed drastically. All the educational systems in China conformed to Communist rules. Karl Marx said all religions were based on ignorance. According to Marx, religion originated in human ignorance and was propagated by ruling castes to maintain their cruel rule. According to the Communists, as workers and peasants stood up to overthrow the ruling class, it was necessary to oppose all religions. The Communists would comb history and science for evidence that supported atheism, translate it, and publish it widely.

I remember that the Chinese Communist government ordered a scientist, not a Christian scholar or Buddhist monk, to be the head of the Department of Religious Affairs in Shanghai when the Communists came into power. The Communists obviously wished to see religions crushed. The students in high schools and colleges were to study "The History of Social Development," which began with the lesson of "From Ape to Man."

I still went to church with my family. The year I graduated from a prestigious university in Shanghai, I was baptized. I often attended young people's meetings. Sometimes, I also was asked to speak in the church, though I was not entirely sure what I believed.

Later, the Chinese government forbade children from going to church, saying it was not good for children to learn about Christianity. The Communists' sinister plan was to stop the propagation of Christianity to the next generation, and it was obvious to everyone who had a mind.

The events of the next few years were agonizing. God was very close to me then, or I could not have withstood the ordeal.

Shortly before the Cultural Revolution began, I had no job and was quite unhappy. Then, one day, my mother said to me that while she prayed and read the Bible, she felt I should read Psalm 121. I had read through the whole Bible several times, and I had listened to many sermons, but I had never paid any special attention to this short psalm. It said:

I lift up my eyes to the hills
where does my help come from?
My help comes from the Lord,
the Maker of heaven and earth.
He will not let your foot slip
he who watches over you will not slumber;
indeed, he who watches over Israel

will neither slumber nor sleep.
The Lord watches over you
the Lord is your shade at your right hand;
the sun will not harm you by day,
nor the moon by night.
The Lord will keep you from all harm
he will watch over your life;
the Lord will watch over your coming and going
both now and forevermore (NKJV).

Not long afterward I returned home one day to a message: Brother Ni Jing-wei, an evangelist in the Pudong district Seventh-day Adventist Church, had come to see me and left word that I should read Psalm 121.

Then, about two weeks later, as my father sometimes went to a Christian Church on Wu-Lu-Mu-Qi road (northern) in Shanghai, the pastor of that church came to our home. Yang Shao-tang was a famous Christian pastor in China. I heard he was originally of the China Inland Mission and had worked with an English missionary, Hudson Taylor. Pastor Yang, my parents, and I had a home worship together. After we sang a Christian song together, Pastor Yang put his eyeglasses on the table in front of him and said, "Read Psalm 121." My father told me to read it aloud. I read the psalm in our Chinese Bible and Pastor Yang explained some things about it. At the end of the home worship, Pastor Yang prayed to God. In his prayer, he repeated the beginning sentences and the last sentence of Psalm 121: "I lift up my eyes to the hills— where does my help come from? My help comes from the Lord, the Maker of heaven and earth. The Lord will watch over your coming and going both now and forevermore."

I was astonished that within about a month three different people had told me to read Psalm 121. If it had been something as well known as Psalm 23 or John 3:16, it might have been a coincidence that three different persons told me to read it within such a short time. Later I met

Brother Ni Jing-wei again and asked him how he thought to tell me to read Psalm 121. He said that he himself felt this psalm to be very good, and he thought he should tell me to read it also.

I concluded that the whole Bible is the inspiration of God to man.

Not long afterward, my father passed away. Some people said it was a mercy of God that my father did not live to see the Revolution. When the Cultural Revolution began, I had two dreams that told me something bad would happen. One of the dreams was that the first floor of our house (the house of my parents has three floors) was confused and some unpeaceful things happened there. Another dream was even more horrible.

Then the Cultural Revolution reached us. First, some students from a nearby middle school came into our house and broke the plates and dishes in our cupboard in the dining room.

Later, more students came and broke all the glass on the doors of our sunroom beside the living room. Then a whole class of students, about 50, from the high school in which my second elder brother worked, came and stationed themselves in our home for more than two weeks. They called the moving company to take away all our tables, sofas, refrigerator, piano, wardrobes, and desks.

After the high school students left, the District Bureau of Houses and Lands decided to let a "worker" family move in to live in a bedroom in our house that had a separate bathroom connected to it, because the Revolutionary Committee of the District Bureau of Houses and lands claimed that ownership of our house had been taken away by the country, as my father had been a capitalist. Our living room and dining room were used by the Production Group of the Revolutionary Committee of the Passages to make cardboard paper. Our family was restricted to living in three small rooms with one bathroom.

According to statistics disclosed later by the government, about 500,000 homes in Shanghai were ransacked during the Cultural Revolution. And about 100 million people were persecuted or affected by the Cultural Revolution in all of China.

Soon I was sent into prison in the District Police Headquarters because the authorities knew that as a Christian, I did not do everything the way "revolutionary people" did, and some "revolutionary people" disliked me. I was imprisoned again during the Cultural Revolution, more than three years altogether. Owing to my providential experience with Psalm 121 just before the Cultural Revolution, I was prepared spiritually. I never wavered in my faith in God. Even during the darkest hours in my prison life, I never denied my faith in Christianity. This was God's grace to me.

After my release from prison, my mother passed away. Mao was still alive, and the Cultural Revolution did not end, though it was not as fierce as it had been. Some more rooms were returned to us by the housing authorities in Shanghai. I started to work in a factory. One night, I had a dream. I saw in the dream that my room was in great confusion, just the way it happened during the first period of the Cultural Revolution, when the Red Guards had come into our house to rummage and ransack. I was worried in the morning when I woke up, because I had not had such a dream since the Cultural Revolution began. I prayed and went out to work.

When I came back in the afternoon, my second elder brother told me that his son had been caught by the police listening to the radio broadcasts from Taiwan with other youngsters.

In the evening, when I was in my room on the third floor of the house, the same brother came up and told me that policemen had come to search my nephew's belongings on the second floor of the house. I was greatly worried. I had just been released from prison and was still despised. It was likely that the policemen would come into my room next. Then I remembered the dream I had the night before. I hurried to take out my secretly kept Bible and some gold rings, etc. left to me by my mother (in those years it was illegal to keep gold things in any private home). I wrapped them up in a bundle, opened the window, and threw the bundle up to the roof. I dared not climb up to the roof, fearing that there might be some guards posted in the passage outside our house. Then I heard the policemen come upstairs and start to search the small room occupied by my second elder brother.

I sat down and turned on my radio to listen to the Japanese Lectures, which taught people the Japanese language. I was greatly worried, and my mind was confused. I could not sit down calmly. So I stood up. I prayed to God, asking Him to help me, and then I opened the door and went out. I saw two policemen standing outside of my second elder brother's room and two other policemen searching in the small room. I said to the policemen that I knew they came for my nephew's matters. I told them that I warned him that he should keep good company. My second elder brother helped me somewhat in telling the policemen that I did not even take my meals with them. One of the policemen said, "You go inside." I hurried back to my room, sitting down to listen to the Japanese Lectures again.

The Lectures went for half an hour on the radio. The search of the small room, which was about 90 square feet in size, went on for about the same amount of time. Then the four policemen left, and I retrieved my things from the roof, thanking God for warning me in advance the night before and protecting me through this dangerous situation. If the policemen had come into my room, it would have looked just as it had in my dream the night before.

After the Cultural Revolution ended, I was officially exonerated by the Police Headquarters that had detained me.

I came to the U. S. in 1989, shortly after the Tian-An-Men Square massacre, to study in graduate school. My wife and our daughter also left China in 1990. I have been a person who worries about my future sometimes. I did not know whether I might get a job after I finished my graduate studies. In 1992, I dreamed I was making test papers for two classes. In 1995, I dreamed I was teaching an undergraduate mechanical engineering course. That is my job now. God led me all along the way.

I serve a living and loving God.

Sam Sih has taught mechanical engineering at Walla Walla College since 1997.

Down to Earth

Jonathan Ponder

Sometimes when I see a big commercial airliner flying overhead, I wonder about the people on board. The plane is cruising at 500 miles per hour—30,000 feet up. It's just a speck—the people are invisible. But I know they are there. And although I do not know who they are or anything about them, I can presume they are very much like me, like people in general: people with the same problems, the same concerns, the same hopes, the same dreams.

Sometimes I'm up in the plane looking down. What do I see? Is it just a blank city grid with empty roads and buildings? Or what about those nameless mountains and forests over there? Are they just pretty scenery? Of course, I know life exists down there—things are going on, life is happening. But from 30,000 feet, it seems pretty remote.

I was struck by this one day as I flew into Portland at the end of Christmas break. Flying up from California into Portland, I passed over Central Oregon, the Bend/Mt. Bachelor area. It is an amazing skyline: Mt. Bachelor, the Three Sisters, Mt. Washington, Black Butte, Three-Fingered Jack, Mt. Jefferson, Mt. Hood, and even, off in the distance, Mt. Ranier, Mt. Adams, and Mt. St. Helens. The view is spectacular, even if the mountains are nameless and unfamiliar. I focused on the base of Mt. Washington, where I had worked as a counselor at Big Lake Youth Camp. I remembered that I had climbed some of those mountains. I had camped and hiked in those forests. I remembered times of great joy and great frustration down there. I remembered relationships I had built with staff and campers. I had lived down there, and now, looking at the whole scene from above, it had special meaning because I had been down there and knew what it was like.

When places and people and events are viewed from a distance, they don't mean that much. They don't touch us. But when we go to a place or live in a place, when we take the time to know a person, or go through an event, we begin to understand. These things become a part of us when we experience them.

When I ask myself, "What is my image of God? What is my perception of God?" I realize it sounds deceptively simple. I know that I believe in God, I pray to God. I plan on serving God in some way for the rest of my life, but who is this God?

God is a huge, transcendent, in many ways unknowable Being who is out there, up there, somewhere. Although the analogy is imperfect, I can compare God to the people up in the plane. I believe God is there, and I can perhaps say some things about who and what He is, but in many ways I cannot even talk. If I could completely understand and explain God, He would cease to be God.

At the same time, however, this huge, transcendent, unknowable God I cannot even talk about somehow funneled Himself down into His creation. He became us both to make Himself better understood and to understand us and what we go through. By having lived on earth, God is able to understand everything about us: the small things and the big things, what it is like to succeed and to fail, to be praised and to be ridiculed, to remember and forget, to be remembered and to be forgotten; what it is like to experience human joy and terrible suffering. By living with us God has experienced and learned things that even He could not have experienced in any other way. My God is a God who understands me because He has lived with me, and now, as I see His example, I am to continue this process of knowing and understanding people that

God started by coming and living on earth. I am to live trying to know and understand people and to give them some sense of what God is like.

An experience that helped me understand God's incarnation more completely was my year as a student missionary. I learned that any time someone works with people from a vastly different culture, especially in a missionary or outreach capacity, it is bound to produce frustration, sometimes anger. It is also bound to produce a hint of what the Incarnation means.

For ten months I lived on a very small dot in the Marshall Islands teaching at a mission school and working in the church with six other student missionaries. We lived and worked closely with the kids in our school. Some of them were at school 12 hours or more a day: classes in the morning, sports after school, in our house at night getting help on homework or just hanging out. They would tell stories, sing songs, teach us about Marshallese culture and language, and we would tell them about America. Although it got frustrating and stressful at times having 10 or 15 kids in our one-room house, it was usually wonderful to live so close to them.

One time we went down to the middle of the island for a one-year-old's birthday party. The biggest parties are always for a kid's first birthday. The whole island was there. We had a huge feast. After eating, we all sang songs as we marched and surrounded the birthday boy. The singing continued and people started dancing. Some of the other missionaries got pulled into the middle of it all. They were jostled around and sprayed with cheap perfume according to Marshallese custom. In the midst of this joy and celebration, I stopped and looked around, and it hit me: "How am I privileged enough to be a part of these people's lives and celebration? And to be an important part in them? I didn't know that this place or these people existed until I got here a few months ago. And they didn't know me or anything about me before then either."

That was one of the positive parts of my experience. There was also the negative side. The same kids we taught and got to know and tried to love did not always show us the love and appreciation that we would have hoped for. Some of the kids we let into our house and had so much fun with turned around and stole things from us. I can remember thinking, "Don't these kids understand that we like them, that we want to help them in any way we can? Why do they repay us this way?" And in some of my more self-righteous moments I would think, "Don't they understand the sacrifice I'm making for them? Don't they realize that I'm giving up a year of my life to spend with them, to teach them, to try to show them God's love?"

I understand now that, in a way, no, they didn't understand and, no, they didn't really care. They may have liked the things I did for them, but they didn't feel any kind of obligation to me for them. In the same way, I often don't understand or seem to care about what Jesus did for me.

This is what the Incarnation of Jesus is all about. It is God being with us, despite the way we treat Him in return, to help us understand him and to understand us. He is not a God who wants to remain up in the plane looking down, not experiencing what He is looking at. He wants to be on the ground, in the dirt, with us. God coming down like this to understand people gives me an example of what I am called to do.

How does this growing understanding of God's Incarnation affect my daily life? I'll tell you that sometimes it affects me and my relationships with others in profound ways, and sometimes people looking at me would never know that I want to pattern my life after Jesus. It's too easy for me sometimes to pretend not to notice people, to fail to take enough interest to get to know a new person. I'm kind of shy and not very talkative, so I struggle with this; but I have a desire simply to know people—to know what makes them who they are, what motivates them or scares them, what they think about God and the big questions of life.

As I think about my image of God, it's exciting because I will always have more to learn. My understanding will always be changing. I pray that as I continue on my quest through life, I will never forget the mystery, the awe, the transcendence of God. I also pray that I will never forget that God has modeled how to live as a human. As I go through life, as I see and meet new people, I pray that I will not be a passive spectator, a casual observer up in the plane, but that I will be down in the dirt, an active participant in knowing people, understanding people, and continuing the work of Jesus.

Jonathan Ponder is a theology and history major at Walla Walla College. This article was originally presented at the WWC student week of prayer, January 1999.

Part of The Advents

Crayons, kids playing,
I find myself praying,
pouring like a gallon
from a tea-
spoon. I wish I would
let you reach me
other ways without

piercing my heart
with a steeple.

—Erik Ulland

Erik Ulland is a biology graduate student at Walla Walla College. He received his bachelor's degree in bioengineering from WWC in 1997.

Compel Them to Come

Eileen Greenwalt

Go out into the highways and hedges,
and compel them to come in,
that my house may be filled.
Luke 14:23

"Would you like me to bring you anything?" I asked
my eighty-four-year-old Dad. I had noticed that his plate
was empty. He and Mother were visiting my family and
had come to the church potluck with me. There was
plenty of food, but Daddy was barely able to walk these
days. Struggling to his feet and using his cane to balance
himself, Daddy could slowly and precariously shuffle
along. But maybe he was still hungry and just didn't want
to make all that much effort amongst strangers to forage
for seconds. "Would you like seconds? Or dessert?"

"Oh, I'm not caring."

I recognized the tone of voice. Flat. Slow. Absent. I
suddenly felt angry at his indifference. His "not caring"
had always flown in the face of my own interests,
enthusiasms, celebrations, sorrows, dreams, and
convictions. I had been shocked and then deeply
disappointed years ago when I discovered he wasn't
planning to attend my high school graduation.

"You aren't coming to my graduation?" I had asked.

"Oh, I'm not caring one way or the other. This isn't

such a big deal, is it? You aren't valedictorian or anything like that, are you?"

And so when I graduated from college halfway across the country, I did not expect him to come. Nor when I got married. I asked him if he was coming, of course, but expected the hesitant noncommittal response, "Oh, I don't know . . . " And I had not urged him. I had scanned his face on too many disappointing occasions for evidence of pride or appreciation or acceptance to risk making myself more vulnerable once again.

Years later I had confronted him with my disappointment and my sense of loss, and he had responded in surprise. "Why, I didn't come because you didn't care whether I came or not!"

So this trip was different. I stubbornly insisted that they come to visit me though I had moved away from the old hometown and it was just assumed that I should be the one to travel back to visit.

Something got into my system and I kept inviting them. For every concern, I rearranged my plan to accommodate the need. Somehow I had invented this drama in my mind that they would come into my world and see me. I wanted them to know me in my life. I wanted them to see me living in my own home with my husband and our two children. I wanted them to sense something of our pace of life, our daily activities, our friends and church and work. And I was already a little sorry I had.

No, I was seriously sorry I had. From the time I had met them at the airport, I had felt guilty. It now felt like I had imposed my invitation upon them. They had seemed so much more frail than when I had seen them in the summer, and Daddy's first remark upon getting into the car at the airport had been, "I'm never going to leave home again."

My intent to draw them into my own life seemed now selfish or at best impulsive. My father in particular was out of his comfort zone as they accompanied me out and about. They were apologetic and ill at ease. "We are just a burden to you." "We just don't get around like we used to." Already this week I had heard on a daily basis the familiar, "Oh, I'm not caring." But as long as I didn't hear a direct "No," I forged ahead.

I had been particularly excited that they visit at this time of year as I was eagerly watching for the blooming of the dogwoods. "Would you like to drive by after supper and see if the dogwoods are blooming yet?"

"Oh, I'm not caring."

I tried to think how to guess what to do next. "Well," I said, "I always drive past the park every couple of days this time of year to see if the dogwoods are out, so if you don't object, I'll take you along." There were no objections.

But there at the potluck, I stood at my father's side and looked at his empty plate. What does it mean—this I'm not caring? I started to turn away and then added, "Daddy, I don't know what that means. I am happy to get you anything you want. But I need you to tell me what I can do."

"Well, I'm just not caring."

A couple of years earlier I met my Dad in Wales where he had grown up as a boy. He had told countless stories of those days when I was growing up, but one I had never heard before was the way one was supposed to behave when offered a courtesy. For example, one was obligated to offer tea to anyone who stopped by one's home. But the guest was obliged to decline such hospitality, knowing it was offered only as a formality. No matter how many times the refreshment was urged, the guest was to remain adamant: "Oh, no thank you. I'm in a hurry this afternoon and can't possibly stay." Only when the hostess put the cup in your hand could you then accept—and then only reluctantly accept—the courtesy, giving all the honor to the hostess and never admitting you had ever been willing to receive. If at any time it was suspected that the guest really wanted to receive, it was considered a shameful thing. I dismissed this bit of "history" as old-fashioned nonsense.

I also recognized how this form of "politeness" had been interpreted in my own upbringing as strict injunctions against "begging." We were never to ask for anything. Even at Grandma's house, where "help yourself" was the rule, we were supposed to decline such presumption. In fact, not asking and not wanting were two sides of the same coin. So was this lifetime of "not caring" his way of "being polite?" And has my lifetime of "not begging" for him to "care" been interpreted as another brand of indifference?

I again turned to go. "Well, I'll have another serving of those enchiladas . . . and a little more green salad, if you really don't mind getting it for me," he said.

"Mind?" I wanted to shout! "Sure!" I said. "I'll be right back."

As I searched for the enchiladas, I reflected on this sad irony. Had my father been waiting all these years for me to compel him to receive my offers of hospitality while I hesitated to offer in fear of further rejections?

And then somewhere between the enchiladas and the lonely figure of my fragile father, I wondered if I had been insisting too emphatically on loving him on my own terms rather than in the language he understood. Had this awkward dance of uncertainty hidden the real love we have held for each other? Perhaps the "second mile" that Jesus spoke of was to remind us that the compelling power of love is always a surprise, one step beyond the expectations of duty, familial obligations, and cultural norms.

The story of the feast of Luke 14 came to my mind: "Go to those who are the outsiders . . . and compel them to come in, that my house may be filled." Outsiders (insecure people like my father and I, people who worry that we won't fit in, who never feel that we truly belong) need to learn to experience the grace that Jesus compels us to receive! We need to see that His grace includes us, invites us in, seats us, and sustains us at the table of God's love—particularly at those times we don't feel that God's love means us.

And we also need to learn how to compel other "outsiders" to receive God's open hospitality, never wearying of well-doing, as Galatians 6:9 says. God wants His house full! He doesn't withdraw from rejection but continues to offer a place at His table. And if it includes me and my dad, it includes you. "Come in! Come in! I have everything all ready! The table is all set, the tea is poured, and I have a surprise for you. Come!"

Eileen Greenwalt taught speech/language pathology at Walla Walla College from 1976 to 1983. She is a communication consultant on the secondary level for the Walla Walla Public School District.

A Community of God's Children

Todd Schoepflin

Having graduated from college as an electrical engineer, I find myself sprinkling my religious language with mathematical and physical metaphors. In engineering, we often talk about the dimensionality of a problem—how many basis vectors are required to characterize a system. In this case, two sets of categories describe my spiritual journey. First, in *Mere Christianity*, C. S. Lewis talks about the three ways we meet God: through prayer, through human interaction, and by partaking of the sacraments. On the other hand, Scott Peck describes the four stages of spiritual growth: chaos, structure, questioning, and mysticism (which is the true beginning).

My freshman year at Walla Walla College was more about fulfilling academic requirements and learning to navigate college than paying attention to spiritual things. As my sophomore year unfolded, I discovered that my new roommate, Brandon Sanders, was always ready to question my status quo, particularly my attitude toward my church and my beliefs in God. I learned that I lacked the courage and voice to speak questions such as, "Does God exist?" "Evil: why?" "Does this universe have meaning?" Brandon audibly expressed the questions of my heart, and he helped me find my own voice.

That year I also took my first philosophy class, and it encouraged me to explore my questions in the Christian context. Despite the demands of the sophomore engineering schedule, I undertook a daily investigation of the good stuff: *Mere Christianity* and then John and Romans. I discovered a nonlinear belief in God. I found God walked with me in the questioning process, although I couldn't prove God by conventional logic.

Meanwhile, I learned that corporate worship could touch my soul. I discovered a discussion-oriented class on Sabbath mornings and started attending irregularly. The give-and-take contrasted sharply with the presentation-style formats I was familiar with. At the end of winter quarter, I experienced an extraordinary alternative to a conventional final exam in my class on the book of Revelation. During this holy final, we marched through the catacombs of the College Church with candles, singing "We are One in the Spirit." After we spoke the entire book by turns, it seemed sad that we should part without breaking bread together like the early Christians.

Major pieces to the puzzle fell into place during my junior year. In Philosophy of Religion I was formally introduced to the two fundamental issues: God's existence and the problem of evil. Writing a short paper on each problem required a massive emotional energy outflow as I attempted to stay in one place philosophically for an entire week. I found solutions I could live with: subjectivity is truth, and the only proof for God's existence is personal experience. Furthermore, rather than wasting energy wondering how God can allow evil, we can actually do things in concert with God to mitigate evil.

Winter quarter found me in the most rigorous academic situation of my life. Existentialism from Professor Janice Staab challenged me. I emerged from that quarter appreciating metaphor, dialectic, Kierkegaard, and Nietzsche. My final Existentialism paper also added to my personal credo: "Christ vs. Zarathustra: who can save?" Even now, I'm grateful I found that (for me) Christ does tie off the end and, in fact, breaks the cycle of the Eternal Return.

Though much of the work was out of the way, I wasn't really aware of it until one spring Sabbath as I sat during the organ prelude at the College Church. Suddenly, I realized I would always believe; God's existence did not need to remain an open question forever! Up to that point, I simply knew I needed a relaxing spring quarter, but now I had permission. In fact, God's grace was calling me out of my personal exploration toward community. For starters, I joined a small worship group. I also joined the Collegiate Chorale and basked in the joy of singing with all the saints in the College Church.

Additionally, I committed to a 1995 summer mission trip. Our group met weekly during spring quarter and then carried out a construction project in Borneo for six weeks. God cleansed my soul as I pushed my body to the limits. I tried to fill my mind with Dietrich Bonhoeffer's *Cost of Discipleship* but could manage little more than a simple faith that God would make everything okay—and even if it wasn't okay, that was okay, too. The local church members there steadily demonstrated this approach to us daily. In sharp contrast, our group had spiritual and social highs and lows. The experience left me with many questions, many good memories, and a growing appetite for community.

Indeed, my two senior years at Walla Walla College enhanced my appreciation of community. During the week, I met in a small three-person worship group. Since my motivation for a singular search had recently fizzled, this was my chance to see God in new ways. In addition, the Sabbath became full of ritual, made even more meaningful by the tight integration with the people I saw during the week. On Friday afternoons, I would typically do homework and then head over to the campus chapel for a prayer group at 5 p.m. Next, I'd join Mike and Keith and Alden Thompson in a Jewish "welcoming of the Sabbath." We'd drink grape juice, read Jewish liturgy, and sing along with the tape on the portable stereo. Next, I'd go to the cafeteria, eat a leisurely meal with friends, and go to vespers at 7:30. Afterwards, we would be the last to leave, often talking in the pews until 10:30, sometimes carrying the conversation outdoors or to a dorm room.

The ritual resumed with Sabbath breakfast followed by either my favorite Sabbath school or choir practice. I still marvel at the wonderful combination of spiritual food and loving acceptance that was nearly palpable in that Sabbath school.

For many, attending a large church is an intimidating experience, but I found increasing joy in worshiping God en masse. Whether I was in the choir or congregation, I found the gathering of all the saints very inspiring. In fact, this sense of "the more people, the better" is probably a major reason why Tuesday chapels became a favorite part of my week. Scanning the huge audience and recognizing most of the friendly faces was very special. Martin Luther King, Jr. chapels were particularly notable experiences. When we sang "We shall overcome" and then "God is on our side," I would look around at the audience. Seeing all of God's children surrounding me confirmed and renewed my belief that the words were true.

Today, I'm beginning to integrate the intellectual, communal, individual, and mystical aspects of my experience of God. I still sometimes entertain questions. I also worry whether my church has lost its pursuit of present truth and cannot claim the community experience of the early Christians. Nevertheless, I am not disheartened and remain committed to re-invigorating my religious tradition. I have answers and tools with which I may live, a community of God's children with whom to live, and a belief that God is on and at all of our sides. Amen.

Todd Schoepflin is a 1997 electrical engineering graduate of Walla Walla College. He is a doctoral student in electrical engineering at the University of Washington.

A Personal God

Steve Pawluk

We didn't wash our Sabbath lunch dishes until after sundown. We didn't attend the theater or go bowling because Ellen White said that our angels would not enter those sorts of establishments with us. We listened to 33 rpm records of Christian recording artists such as Del Delker and The King's Heralds on Friday evenings. Christmas celebration, with its pagan origins, was one of the many things left behind when my parents converted from European Catholicism to European Seventh-day Adventism. We attended church every Sabbath, sitting faithfully in the fourth row on the left. The preacher could count on it. We witnessed to others like the "watchman on the walls of Zion" so that the blood of unbelievers would not be on our heads (see Ezekiel 3:7-21). Some might say that we were ultraconservative Seventh-day Adventists, but we were merely being faithful and devout.

Then, in the 1970s, I joined a new brotherhood that proclaimed the gospel of peace and love. Along with thousands of other counterculturists, I sought to "find myself." We guarded our individuality by rebelling against The Establishment. It took a few years for the realization to hit me: I was still a conformist and my new church had group standards too. "Make love, not war," was the church's creed. Rock concerts were our worship services. We had a dress code: ragged jeans, tie-dyed T-shirts, scraggly beards, and long hair. We looked and acted pretty much alike in our protesting individuality. The group disdained materialism, and many members held all things in common. Believers were supposed to enjoy Joan Baez, Bob Dylan, the Doors, and the Rolling Stones. And again, I was one of the faithful witnesses. I resisted the draft and, at my senior class night at my Adventist high school, I played the electric guitar for our band while belting out the words of the protest song, "I Feel Like I'm Fixin' to Die Rag." The school didn't allow class nights for three years after that one.

In all the experimenting, I hadn't "found myself" at all. I had merely changed denominations, substituting one type of groupthink for another. Then, one day, as part of a college assignment, I read these words in a book written by the Adventist author Ellen White: "Every human being, created in the image of God, is endowed with a power akin to that of the Creator—individuality, power to think and to do" (*Education*, p. 17). A few lines later I found the oft-quoted, but little contemplated, phrase about being "thinkers, not mere reflectors of other men's thoughts." And I began to contemplate God's design for us, which led me to carefully study The Book. I read it on its own terms. Temporarily setting aside commentaries and study helps as well as previous beliefs, I tried to block out preconceived ideas and to let the picture unfold as though I were reading the Bible for the first time.

Along the way I found for myself that Scripture's primary truths made good sense. I found that the Cross, the Sabbath, and the state of the dead provided valuable pictures regarding the character of God and the essential nature of His universe. I learned that the Ten Commandments and the Sermon on the Mount not only were worthy of many more years of study and analysis, but of emulation in today's world as well. I discovered the benefits of tithing and consistent prayer. And I found relevance in the creation story and the promise of a new creation.

I also discovered that the Body of Christ, while it has only one Head, is made up of individual parts (see

Romans 12, I Cor. 12). The hand is not the eye, and the eye is not the hand. One examines, searches, and discriminates; the other grasps, carries, and pushes. To be sure, the eye sometimes sees things to help the hand avoid injury. Conversely, the hand can learn Braille if the eye gets damaged. But by and large, they share neither appearances, natures, nor functions; but the goal or allegiance to the head is common to all. In fact, even a pair of hands, though they seem much alike, come at things from opposite sides. Vision, to have depth, requires two eyes to view things from different angles. We refer to people who have missing or nonfunctioning parts as disabled or challenged. I imagine a church where we all try to play the same part, attempting to think and function alike, might be considered disabled and spiritually challenged too.

This metaphor has helped me understand that only in Christ's design are diversity and individuality fully valued. Current society tries to make sure we all drink Pepsi, drive Chevrolets, and wear Levis. But God calls us to be individuals, thoroughly enjoying the Creator's gifts of the power to think creatively and to do accordingly. And so my Christian walk has become intensely personal in recent years. I've tried vigorously to resist bandwagons and groupthink. Individual study and devotion times allow me to be in touch with the Source of creativity. Conversing with God, one to One, has given me confidence in my beliefs and values. My faithfulness is measured by God's word, not by accountability to a program.

There is, to be sure, great value in comparing perspectives with others. Reality checks can be very helpful. After all, when the nose reports sniffles, the joints of the hand can confirm a flu with their own aches, or suggest, by reporting no flu symptoms from their areas of the body, that a more accurate diagnosis may be allergies or merely brisk outside temperatures. When the mouth speaks, the ears hear, and the person determines whether he really means what he has said. When the feet run, the arms provide counterbalance so the body doesn't fall in its haste. Likewise, individuals' perspectives of Truth can be adjusted or confirmed by comparing experiences and probing the convictions of the other members of the body. But the nose and the hand do not necessarily need to have the same experience or opinions. I imagine that the nose and the hand don't even share all of the same values. The members communicate. The members empathize. The members cooperate when it is beneficial to do so. But they remain individual members.

Our God is infinite; His Truth must be large enough to include various perceptions of reality and various expressions of our devotion to God in lifestyle and worship. Consider that even in prayer, the eyes close while the hands open to God. In worship, the mouth actively expresses its adoration, but the ears prefer to listen quietly and passively. The body of Christ is a model of unity in diversity, designed so the Head can be served in many ways. The greater the diversity, the more complete the service of the body. This is radically counter to earthly organizations and systems, which demand conformity and even uniformity of their members. Even the "Sometimes you Gotta Break the Rules" message of Madison Avenue seeks to compel us to break the rules in the same way, its way.

Perhaps this is why Jesus admonished us to pray and give alms in private. Maybe this is why He taught us not to let even the left hand know what the right hand is doing (see Matthew 6). It is difficult for me to believe that, when Jesus said these things, He was just presenting clever, entertaining metaphors. I'm increasingly convicted that these commandments contain vital truths. While organizations appear to have consistently ignored these teachings, Jesus challenges us to have the courage to experience a personal religion and an intensely individual expression of our relationship with God. There must be important reasons for this, perhaps having to do with the nurture of our individual commitments to God, ensuring a diversity of ministries in a world with many different needs and protecting our "spiritual gene pool" from excessive inbreeding.

I am still exploring the meaning and best use of that tremendous power that the Creator gave to us, the power of individuality, the power to think and to do. I am grateful to God, however, that He trusted us with that capacity and designed a universe that functions best with diverse ideas of perspective, of expression, and of worship. For now, at least, my spiritual journey is focused on the cultivation of my private relationship with God, nurturing independence of thought, and making my singular contributions to the body of Christ. While doing so, I'll seek to understand your perspectives and to appreciate your uniqueness as we each respond to the mind of the creative and infinite One. And as we grow, we will want to compare notes along the way.

Steve Pawluk is professor and chair of education at Walla Walla College, where he has taught since 1991.

The Patience of God

Martha Mason

During my junior year at the University of Illinois, I was disfellowshipped from the church of my childhood. It was a conservative Seventh-day Adventist church of the 50s and 60s, so my folk dancing, jewelry, and moviegoing were glaring signs to the small Midwestern congregation that I was in open rebellion against God. Although I didn't see my lifestyle as leaving out God in any conscious way, it was true that I had not kept a close relationship with Jesus. My church did not have much to say about grace, and few of us knew that God's unconditional love and acceptance do not hinge on social and cultural customs that can vary with time and place. So I believed, along with my fellow churchgoers, that the unacceptable things I wanted to do somehow naturally had separated me from God.

Still, after the church elders visited that day, I felt deeply hurt. I felt alienated, alone, yet unwilling to change without what I thought were good reasons. I told myself I would never go back to church. Later, I would think about church in passing, but I felt nothing. I was disappointed, though, that I had lost my God and the Sabbath celebration I had always enjoyed.

I fell into the political and social revolutions of the 60s fairly easily. They offered plenty of support for people like me who felt disenfranchised from organized religion. Unfortunately, my first marriage became a casualty in part of this upheaval in society. But the breakup was also an opportunity for me to begin to think for myself. Eastern religions had drawn me ever since I had traveled and lived in Asia. I lost touch with Christianity, and I stayed away from the relatives I thought would pester me about religion.

Fifteen years passed, and then I received word that my foster father had died. He had been a powerful spiritual force in my early life, and I knew I must break my long separation from the family and go to the funeral. Part of me did not want to go. I was afraid people would hassle me about my beliefs and lifestyle, but I was even more afraid that in my emotional weakness I might not be honest about my present lifestyle and beliefs. So partly as self-defense and definitely as a statement, I put on my largest earrings and caught a bus from San Francisco to Sacramento.

There to meet me was my foster brother, a kind man who was both liberal and loyal to the church. I knew he would feel no obligation to set me straight. He and his wife made it clear that they still loved me.

We drove together to a smaller town for the funeral service. There, most uncomfortably, I had to take part in the final ritual that highlighted a faith to which I could no longer subscribe. During the service people were kind to me. Amazingly, not a negative word was said about my appearance. I was apparently being received in the family as if nothing were amiss.

Although tentatively relieved, I kept on guard. When the burial time came, we rode to yet a smaller town with a tiny, old cemetery on top of a wooded hill. We assembled on the dry turf while the pastor spoke informally with my mother in an unusual kind of conversation homily about the resurrection day. Listening carefully and tearfully, I decided I couldn't be part of that conversation. I didn't belong on resurrection morning, I told myself. I was sure I would have to miss that day, to skip the glory and sight of God because I was a rebel.

My foster brother drove me back to the bus, keeping our talk gently light, and the kindness of his voice was a balm to some ache I could not express. When I got back to the city that night, I couldn't find one earring. It had been lost in the shuffle of travel and hugs.

I started thinking about God again. I think I missed Him in my life without my foster father in the world anymore. Perhaps these longings were in the air around me: the *San Francisco Chronicle* ran an article about how scientists were saying mankind could be reduced chemically to the constituents in mud. I heard Christmas songs on the radio. The twin towers of the big church across the street were lit up in blue for a holy day. Sometimes these things brought me tears, and my memories turned to the God of my childhood. Most of the time, though, I still read about Buddhism and continued to see it as humane and reasonable.

My Bible seemed to look at me, almost trembling there on the shelf where I had placed it years earlier. I was afraid even to look at it. But one day when thinking about my birth mother (I was not raised by her), I recalled that she was a Nazarene. The thought that she had been a Christian touched me at that moment. I took down my Bible. I reasoned that the Nazarene, a somehow friendly-sounding word, might be kind to me. I allowed myself to read in the Gospels for a little while.

What happened then was a strange surprise. I rather realistically "saw" a kindly face and presence on the pages as I read. It was a warm source of comfort. I continued several of these times of Bible reading, but quit later when I came across a difficult text. I went back to reading Buddhism.

I met my first Christian friend in the city—Frieda. We had a lot in common, including Dutch heritage and a very strict Christian upbringing. Her laughter was a language of hope that I wanted to hear. It seemed to come from the depth of her courageous experience where she had battled conservative legalism but had never given up on God. We kept in touch.

Some time later, I awoke in the middle of a sound

sleep, hearing a strong "voice" saying "You could go back to church!" I knew that it was probably an angel talking to me, which shook me up. I didn't know what to think, but from this time on, a series of dreams came to me that I could only interpret as God trying to get my attention.

As a result of "the voice," I started to attend church. I went a couple of times with Frieda. Also, since I had always wanted to go to some of the grand old picturesque churches around the city, I started visiting around. I was also under the influence of other Christians: Anna, a delightful Catholic woman, and Andre, a Chinese Southern Baptist.

I looked at my Christian friends with curiosity: they were reasonably intelligent and well-adjusted, and they seemed to enjoy life heartily. Why were they believers in something unseen and a religion that centered on a bloody event? The answer did not come about logically. It took some slow turning in my mind and subtle working on my spirit before I could soften toward God. I contrasted what I felt when reading Buddhism. I started to find it a disappointment not to find a personal God there in the way I had sensed in the Gospels.

An Adventist woman, Alice, began to work in my office. Her workplace was right beside mine, and in a short time I told her I had been raised Adventist but was not a Christian anymore. It felt cold to say it, but I knew I could not honestly say otherwise. She almost seemed not to hear what I was saying; at least she was not offended. She began a chatty relationship with me about many other things that did not exclude me. She was nice, but something about her began to upset me—she caused me to think about my position, sitting on the fence. It became difficult for me to talk to her, and I tried to avoid her even when she seemed to seek me out. Soon I got a job in a different department. I didn't see Alice at all any more, except in passing.

The boss in my new department, Dwayne, was a local

"character." He was a gregarious Swede who wore clogs. He was also a Christian—Evangelical Covenant. He was the active sort, the kind who mentions Christianity often. I thought he was especially nice, but I told him clearly I was not a believer. He seemed to pay little attention to that but instead invited me to attend a Good Friday service with him.

I was afraid. Christian music made me cry, and I didn't know if I believed "all that." I reluctantly said "No" to Dwayne, but something inside me said I should go to church that weekend and deal with the confusion I felt.

I thought about the Adventist church downtown, right in the center of the city. It was a wonderful old building with turn-of-the-century "carpenter gothic" design. It also had a beautiful stained glass window of Christ talking to a woman, probably Mary Magdalene. I sneaked in incognito. It was very strange because no one seemed to be in the church. All the doors were open, but I saw no one. I walked up the steep stairs inside and peered into the sanctuary.

Then I paused at the literature rack. I looked, puzzled, and then I panicked. There I saw my problem: flames leaped up from the cover of one pamphlet—it was an illustration of the final burning of the world, a visualization of Hell. I could not come to terms with the violence, the blood, the flames. Was God in all this? Before anyone could materialize, I dashed out on to the street, safe. I remember being glad that I could go shopping in Chinatown, in an atmosphere where there was no pressure on my soul.

The night I turned down Dwayne's Easter invitation, I thought about my earlier, solitary church visit and about the issue of scripture, the story of God from beginning to end— yes, even an awful end. It was wildly uncomfortable. Yet here at Easter all the world—at least many in my world— were believing it. I thought of Christ. Did I believe in Him? What about the Cross? I couldn't answer these questions.

I decided I ought to clear up these issues and to attend church on Saturday. I had already learned that I was not totally comfortable in churches that worshiped on Sunday. I had been unable to find a Bible basis for Sunday worship.

The experience I had that Sabbath changed my life. Instead of some emotional crisis and collapse, I felt something else. As I listened to the Easter story from the pulpit—not an "inspirational" or outstanding sermon but rather a very low-key and reasoned one—I realized that my problem was simple. At that moment I said to myself that in fact I did believe in Jesus, that I wanted him to be reality for me, that I did believe the scripture story. It was an incredible quiet moment of feeling suddenly "at home" and at peace.

After that day some great things and some terrible things took place. But the power that possessed me in that moment of belief was greater than my needs, and it has kept with me continuously, sustained me, and confirmed me beyond my wildest dreams.

I credit Christian friends. None of them preached. They lived, went to church, and enjoyed life. I credit my assortment of faithful Christian relatives who were generous to a fault and who were people of faith and love. I credit the church family I found in the City that loved me in the "rough"—it took me some time to understand what righteousness by faith is about, and I'm still working out the details. I credit all of the people who accepted me with unconditional love. Most of all, I credit the great and patient power of God to speak personally in ways I would finally hear, eventually listen to, and gradually think about—learning to trust, to love, and finally to submit.

Martha Mason is an assistant professor of art at Walla Walla College, where she has taught since 1995.

The Woman at the Well

Beverly Beem

THE WOMAN INTRODUCES HERSELF:

I don't know how you good folks could have heard about me, unless it was from that book that John wrote, the one about Jesus. You must have read it. Remember? I am the Vine. I am the Bread. "I am the Way, the Truth, the Life." There's no doubt about it. It just grabs my heart.

And not least of all because I am in it. Can you believe it? Me? Of all the hundreds of conversations that Jesus had, of all the thousands of people that Jesus met, John would tell about me. I can't hide the fact that I'm as pleased as punch about that.

But does something strike you a little strange about the way John tells my story? Did you notice? John is telling my story. And he leaves out my name! Thirteen times. Count them. Thirteen times he calls me "The Woman." You would think that just once he could slip in my name, like it would destroy the narrative flow or something.

Well, before we go any further, I want you to know my name. My mother did not call me The Woman at the Well. I have an old and honored name among my people. My name is Tamara.

I bet some of you know what this feels like. You don't have names either. You, too, are the Girl. The gal, the guy. But, you know something, Jesus knew my name. And I am here to tell you about the day that I met Jesus.
COMING TO THE WELL:

I came to the well late that day. All right. So. I came to the well late that day. For twenty centuries, male commentators have been making hay over that. She came late to the well. Now, let's see—They scratch their erudite heads. What can we make of that?

How many reasons can you think of why a person might be running late? Do you want to hear what they come up with? I'll tell you. I have been collecting their comments for years. I've got a file. I don't mean to brag, but, well, the truth is, I am a bit of a scholar. So, here they are, why the woman was late to the well.

She's a social outcast.

She's too ashamed to be seen in public.

She doesn't get along with the other women.

And how can they say all this stuff about my character? Well, She's been Married Five Times. TSK. TSK.

Gar-bage. All of it. Slander is what it is. I want you to know that I am an important and influential person in my community. I have ideas about things, and I speak my mind. And people listen to me, too. Social Outcast. My hind foot.

Do you want to know why I came late to the well that day? I'll tell you.

It was Divine Providence. That's what it was. Have you ever read that in any of your commentaries? But think about it. The Word was made Flesh. Right? That's what John says. Well, I'm here to tell you that the Flesh was thirsty. Now, would the heavenly Father sit up there on his throne and let his Son dry up and blow away in the desert heat? I think not. So, he comes down, and he looks through all the city of Sychar, and he picks out me. And he guides me through my day until I arrive at just the right place at just the right moment to give his Son a drink of water when he needs it. Stuff that in your commentaries.

These guys are just like the disciples. I'll never forget the look on their faces when they come back and find Jesus and me deep in conversation. Jesus is telling me things he has been trying to tell them for years. But they don't get it. They don't know what he's talking about. But I get it. I know what he's talking about. I had been studying the prophecies for years. All my life, I had been getting ready for this conversation.

But do they see any of that? They do not. All they see is—"The Woman." And their brains spin into neutral. Their thought processes screech to a halt. They reach into their grab bag of stereotypes and pull out "Slut," and in a moment, they have me boxed, labeled, and shipped out the door.

But Jesus didn't put me in any box. He didn't slap me with any labels.

THE WOMAN MEETS JESUS:

I hardly noticed him at first. He was sitting by the well. Alone. Hot. The sun beating on his head. Thirsty. Clearly thirsty. I would gladly have given him a drink right then and there, but I didn't dare. I was a woman. I couldn't do anything to help him. Just to look at him could be taken as an insult. So, tough luck, man. I just fixed my gaze on the horizon and went about my work.

And then I heard his voice. He was speaking to me. I looked up. He was looking at me. And when my eyes met His, they didn't dart away.

"Give me a drink," he said. Just like that. Like it was the most natural thing in the world. He was thirsty. I had water. So . . . Give me a drink.

It took me a minute to recover myself. This man had just toppled two social barriers like the walls of Jericho to speak to me. No way was I going to hand him a drink of water and watch him ride off into the sunset. I had to know who he was.

So, I'm not shy. I come right out and ask him. "What's the deal? How come you, a man, ask help of me, a woman? How come you, a Jew, speak to me, a Samaritan?"

You know, his eyes sort of brightened at my questions. He looked at me more intently, and while he drank water from my pitcher, he began to talk about God and worship. And the things that touched my heart. And the things that touched his heart.

And as we talked, I began to think, "This is no ordinary man." He must be a prophet. And then the more we talked, I began to think, "This is no ordinary prophet." And then, cold chills began to run up and down my spine. Is it possible? Could it be?

Well, there are some things you can't just come right out and ask. "Nice chatting with you, might you be the Messiah?"

So, I come at it obliquely. I can be quite diplomatic when I need to be. I make a side reference to the Messiah. I just toss it in, cool-like, into the conversation. I open the door just a crack and stand back to see what he will do. And he takes that door and throws it wide open. "I that speak unto you am he."

"I that speak unto you am he." Not: I who raise the dead. Or: I who heal the sick. Or: I who walk on water.

But, I, who speak to you. I, who knock down the barriers between men and women, between peoples. That is the I who is the Messiah.

Those were the last words he said to me. Just then, the disciples returned. And all meaningful dialogue was at an end.

THE DISCIPLES RETURN:

Suddenly we were engulfed in this swarm of disciples. They just glared at me. With Jesus there, they didn't dare say a word; but oh, if looks could kill. Puzzled looks. Angry looks. Indignant looks that The Woman dare speak to their personal private Messiah.

I just glared back. It was not a Kodak moment. I know, I wasn't helping the situation any. I knew what I was supposed to do. I was supposed to cover my face and avert my eyes and hang my head in the face of this bank of masculinity. But, you know. I just couldn't do that. I had spent the last hour looking on the face of Christ. I was now a disciple. And no one, not even another disciple, would ever make me hang my head.

So, I looked away from those hostile faces and turned my eyes on Jesus. Then it was my turn to drop my mouth open in amazement. This was not the same Man I had first seen at the well. I had seen a man slumped over in exhaustion. This man was charged with energy from head to toe. And his whole face was lit up with one huge grin.

And as I looked into his eyes, I saw him give me a nearly imperceptible nod, and I knew exactly what I had to do. I was not just a disciple. I was a commissioned apostle. I dropped my pitcher and ran full speed back to Sychar.
SYCHAR:

The first person I met was an elder of the city, an official in our temple. A good person, like me, waiting for the Messiah. "He is here," I said. "It has got to be him. It can be no other. You have to come and see for yourself. We all do. Everyone. You go to the North side of the city. I'll take the South side. We will meet in the center."

We didn't miss a soul. Up and down the streets we went, banging on doors, calling out to our neighbors. Over and over and over again, I told my story of how I met Jesus, of all he had said. "Come, the Messiah is here. You must see him for yourself. You must hear him for yourselves."

And when I marched back to the well, I was leading the entire city of Sychar behind me. And you know what I was thinking? I am almost too embarrassed to tell you. But I was thinking—"What if he's not there? What if he's gone?" What if the disciples have yanked him along on their journey? What if—and this made my blood run cold—what if he has given up on me? It had been some time. What if he thought I wasn't coming back?

But I needn't have worried. He was at the well where I had left him, waiting for me and for whomever I might

bring back with me. And when he saw me break over the horizon, with the entire city of Sychar—men, women, children, and household pets, looming up behind me, he threw back his head and his laughter filled the skies.
JESUS AND THE WOMAN MEET AGAIN:

Once again Jesus and I met at the well. Once again Jesus and I were surrounded by a swarm of people. This time happy, laughing people, all eager to meet Jesus, all eager to hear him, to see him, to touch him and to be touched by him.

I introduced him to every person by name. He spoke each name. Held each hand. Looked into each face. Spoke to each heart. We couldn't let him go. We never did let him go.

I don't know when I will see Jesus again. It may well be in his kingdom—that kingdom of spirit and truth he told me about. And when I see him, I know, he will be surrounded by a crowd of disciples. But do you know what I am going to do? I am going to take my pitcher and fill it to the brim with cool, clear, sparkling water. And I am going to bust through that crowd of disciples, and I am going to hand it to him, and I am going to say, "Remember me?"

I wish to thank Elaine Giddings from Andrews University who introduced me to The Woman at the Well and told me her name.

Beverly Beem is professor and chair of the Walla Walla College English department, where she has taught since 1976.

The Sacred Clown,
The Buffoon and The Christian

an excerpt from an ongoing research project looking at what the Christian
Community can learn from a community of artists

Kimberly Howard

In the beginning was the Word and the Word was with God, and the Word was God. He was with God in the beginning. Through him all things were made; without him nothing was made that has been made. In him was life, and that life was the light of men. The light shines in the darkness, but the darkness has not understood it. (John 1: 15, NRSV)

Art is metaphor. It is a representation of life. It is not life. It is not pretending to be life; it is the essence of the truth of life, because the artist creates it, including in the creation the experience of living: love, loss, victory, and pain. And still it is representation. Still it is not life. Still it is only as much as the artist knows to be truth. And included are the questions. When writing an article on Christianity and Art I must say that in my search for truth, I seek to find where one, art, can benefit the other, Christianity. My art is theatre. I call myself a Christian. I speak from what I know. The artisans in the theatre speak of their art in this way:

"A theatre that makes no contact with the public is irrelevant."

". . . [theatre] played to the benefit of the crowd, not to please them."

"A role is ready only when the actor has made the words of the character his own words . . . then the emotion will speak from the essence, which is the most valuable and only convincing and genuine sort."

I often, without realizing, substitute church, spirituality, God and religion into the above quotes. In this way are my Christianity and my art linked, each one inspiring the other, learning from the other.

If Christianity can learn from art, it's because the metaphors of art are larger than we are—as it is with spirituality. Representation changes the crowd. It changes behavior. Standing outside self helps us, because of the distance it creates, to see the truth of life. Van Gogh's *Starry Night* is what we see and what he sees when he looks at the night. It is not a replica, or a perfect reproduction of what God created; it is a view of the night through the eyes of the artist. Because of the barrier of the art—theatre, painting, music, poetry—and the alienation that comes with it, the intensification of the human experience, we can see it more clearly. Borrowing from the ideas of Bertolt Brecht, the 1930s German theatre director, alienation helps us view ourselves without the lie of mimicry. The characters know what we know. They show us to ourselves, and we see more than we ever could without them. Characters from the theatrical tradition stand side by side with the parables.

Enter the sacred clown—let's call her Dijinn. She is the traveler. She is on a spiritual journey, in search of truth. Her story is our own, students, philosophers, those leading an examined life and following the way, questioning the way. On her travels she tells the story of her spiritual leader. She is ever discovering, there is naivete in her movements, her studies, her thoughts. This she shares with others on her way. She is the caretaker of the sacred stories; there is freedom and timelessness in her walk.

Enter the buffoon—let's call him the actor. He is a traveler. He is an outcast in search of community and truth, or truth in community. His story is the story of the artist, one leading an examined life and following the way, questioning the way. On his travels he tells the story of his journey, of being cast out of society, of living on the fringe: he is wise beyond humanity; he plugs into every experience fully and without inhibition. To the buffoon nothing is sacred. This profanity is what enables him to be heard, for others do heed him; his is the truth held up to us through ourselves. He is a teacher, and mirror, reflecting our mistakes, our arrogance, and our deepest fears.

Enter the Christian—let's call him the Pharisee. He is a traveler. He is in the world, but not of the world. He has the truth. His truth is the Bible. His truth is the Lord, Jesus Christ. His truth is the Sabbath, the Second Coming, and the spirit of prophecy. His story is the story of the wayfarer who has lost his way on this earth and seeks a heavenly reward. On his travels he tells the story of his spiritual awakening; he warns fellow travelers that the way to truth is narrow. Everything that is of the church is sacred, everything else profane; a story with a Christian moral is sacred, no matter how artless the form which carries it. He too is a teacher, but he has forgotten his calling, forgotten his task; because he already knows the answers, there is nothing left to discover.

The life of art is the life of the continual journey in search for truth. The starry night, tonight, is not the same one of tomorrow or of yesterday. The early Adventists believed in the discovery, openly defying the status quo in their search for truth. Yet, a system frozen in time, to borrow a phrase from a colleague, is one doomed to fail; with structure comes tyranny, with tyranny comes complacency. We need to continue to embark on a journey of discovery in order to find truth, because the light has come into the world and the darkness has not understood it. We are arrogant to assume otherwise.

> It means that we attack one another, that we
> may collide; it means that we may argue, doubt
> each other, offer alternatives. It means that I
> may feel foolish or unprepared. It means that
> rather than blindly fulfilling instructions, we
> examine choices in the heart . . . through repetition and
> trial and error (Anne Bogart, theatre director).

Define the metaphor how you will. The truth is yours to discover.

Kimberly Howard taught drama at Walla Walla College from 1995-1999. This article first appeared in Scanner Magazine.

A Supple Grace

Ron Jolliffe

We were invited to the Hughies' for Sabbath dinner
and I was scared. The Hughies were rich and we were
poor. The fact that Mr. Hughies was a banker and his wife
an attorney never entered into my calculation as an eight-
year-old. I simply knew that my father drove a logging
truck and my mother was a housewife. Dad's income was
theoretically good, but seasonally adjusted. Spring
flooding wiped out logging roads. Summer fire season
shut down the woods for weeks on end. Winter snows
closed landings. In the fall, striking lumber and wood-
products workers closed the mills. And then when
everything was going well in the industry, the log truck
broke down.

We arrived after church at the Hughies' door. Well,
here we were, about to be exposed as the country
bumpkins I believed us to be. Dad rang the door bell. The
Hughies lived in a new house at the end of a row of
custom-built estate homes. They were new to our church,
and I supposed they hadn't yet discovered they were
inviting a family with impoverished social skills. Don
Hughies answered. He was nine and knew so much about
the world. We played with his miniature train set while
dinner was being prepared. I was surprised that his
locomotive didn't come (like mine) with a glass dropper
and bottle of liquid to make the smokestack belch and
wheeze like the train on *Gunsmoke*. Perhaps poor boys had
some things rich boys didn't.

I was just beginning to enjoy myself when we were called to dinner. When I saw the dining room table I was terrified. It was elegantly set with multiple spoons and forks, stemware and cloth napkins. I had no idea what to do with any utensils beyond the basic fork, knife and spoon that surrounded the Melmac at home. I had only seen tables set like this in magazines at the eye doctor's office. The Hughies ate like the people in the magazine and I felt paralyzed. In panic, I sat where Mr. Hughies instructed, curling left thumb in right hand to cover the wart at the first knuckle. Mr. Hughies said grace while I clamped my eyes behind my glasses.

But Mrs. Hughies knew how to make me feel at ease. She moved with grace and beauty. She was the first woman to catch my eye in some inexplicable way. Her hand moved with supple elegance as she spoke. She eased my discomfort by treating me as a confidant, telling me I didn't have to have any casserole if I didn't want any, because she remembered how much she disliked casseroles when she was my age. Timidly I said I'd try some. She smiled. Without hurry those elegant fingers served me casserole. From her simple actions at dinner, I learned the most fundamental meaning of grace. Grace is not a doctrine. It is the experience of being understood and accepted, warts and all. As always, I learned more from grace shown than the grace said.

Ron Jolliffe is a professor of biblical studies at Walla Walla College, where he has taught since 1989. He is a 1971 graduate of WWC.

WINTER QUARTER

Where can I go from your Spirit?
　　Where can I flee
　　from your presence?

If I go up to the heavens,
　　you are there;
　　if I make my bed
　　in the depths,
　　you are there.

If I rise on the wings of the dawn,
　　if I settle on the far side
　　of the sea,

even there your hand
　　will guide me,
　　your right hand
　　will hold me fast.

If I say, Surely the darkness
　　will hide me
　　and the light become
　　night around me,

even the darkness
　　will not be dark to you;
　　the night will shine like the day,
　　for darkness is as light to you.

　　　　　　　　　Psalm 139:7-12, NIV

A Story of Divine Wrath

Glen Greenwalt

"Stevie, Stevie, why did you do it? Oh my boy, oh my boy, why did you do it?" The first drops of rain splattered on our windshield as I drove out of the cemetery. In the rearview mirror, my uncle stood silhouetted over the mound of fresh earth he refused to leave. To the east the sky had turned a dark purple, as it can during a summer thunderstorm in Montana. In the distance, up along Pine Ridge, where it had happened less than a week before, bolts of lightning hurtled down from the darkened sky.

To the casual viewer, a Montana thunderstorm is a spectacular sight, but to farmers and those burying their dead, thunderstorms are dark omens.

"It doesn't look good," I said, watching the already-ripening wheat waving wildly in the fields alongside the road.

"Why does it have to rain just now?" my mother replied. "It is hard enough for Gene to leave his boy in that grave, let alone to have it rain."

Years before, as a small child, I had early learned to read the signs of the weather. I remember dancing joyfully as the wind and rain beat against our window, and I chanted, "It's raining, it's pouring, the old man is snoring . . ." That day my father had cut me short, pointing out the obvious adult fact—the storm outside was destroying our year's livelihood.

Today, I was learning that storms can portend losses more important than crops.

*****

Almost three decades have passed, and the scene out my rearview mirror is as vivid as the everyday view outside my office window. Hardly a week goes by that I don't think of my uncle's sorrow. Each holiday, each major transition of my life, each moment I look forward to, I still see my uncle standing over the country grave of his son and hear the refrain of his words. Within hours of the accident, my grandfather had called and told my dad that he should go down to Hardin, my parents' childhood home town fifty miles to the south, and talk to Gene immediately. My grandfather never much appreciated my father's religion, except in times like these. He feared his daughter had married some religious fanatic, since my father was a Seventh-day Adventist. On the day of the accident, he was simply afraid that Gene might lose his mind. So my parents left almost immediately to comfort my uncle, while my sister and I finished the farm chores.

When my sister and I got to Hardin the next day, my father told me that Uncle Gene was in the other room and that I should go and say something.

He was sitting in an armchair, holding a large family Bible. The weight of the Bible was comforting him, not the words, for his head tilted back while he stared bleary-eyed at the ceiling.

"Hi, Glennie-boy," my uncle addressed me, despite my twenty years, when his eyes finally focused on me. (Somehow, on my mother's side of the family, diminutive endings hung on long after they were dropped by other families.) "My God, you've grown. You're already a man."

"I'm-m-m sorry," I stammered incoherently, saying what I had rehearsed. "It must be hard."

My uncle gave what I took to be a nod and retreated back into his silence.

"You know what is so really hard . . . ?" he finally said. His question trailed off into another long silence . . . "I always pictured Stevie coming home for Christmas with my first grandchild. . . ."

To understand a line like that requires seeing my grandfather's movies. He purchased one of the first home movie cameras and believed that one had to move the camera continually to make "movies." He took "movies" of only two things—his cattle and the grandchildren at Christmas. (Today, most of his grandchildren have left the farm, so once a year at Christmas we take out our video cameras, and *holding them very still,* we take pictures of our children opening their gifts—all of us, that is, except Steve.)

In those old movies we are still young and invincible. My grandfather took reels of film of us grandchildren—specially of Steve and his brother Doug—jumping off things. My grandfather liked projecting these pictures in reverse to hear our glee as we leaped backward up onto couches, porches, and even haystacks. The one picture we never saw, however, was that of Steve jumping up onto haystacks. Steve had asthma, so he couldn't be around the hay. It's clear from the movies that asthma was dangerous to Steve, but we never thought much about it back then.

*****

I first learned how it happened from my grandmother, in her heavy German accent.

"*Ach*, I don't know. You know Stevie had asthma. Gene and the hired man were stacking hay that day, so Stevie was working around the yard, instead.

"Tell me Glennie, what gets into kids' heads? Gene warned him never to go swimming up in those water holes, but his cousin came by and talked him into going swimming with him, so they drove up to Pine Ridge, and the next thing Gene knows his nephew is out at the haystack yelling up at him that Stevie's drowned.

"I guess, Gene just went crazy . . . He was plumb out of his mind . . . *Ach*, he can't even swim, but he races up to those water holes and grabs a piece of waterlogged wood, and paddles around looking for Stevie, crying out, 'Stevie, Stevie, oh my boy, where are you?'"

"*Ach du lieber*, he was just plumb crazy. No one could stop him. Stevie is drowned, and now my son who can't swim is paddling around hanging onto a piece of fence post. I could have lost a grandson and a son. Think about that. A grandson and a son . . . *Ach du lieber*."

*****

On the day of the funeral we arrived early, but already people were standing outside the mortuary. Steve's death appeared to be the whole town's loss.

Just before the service, six husky high school boys filed in and sat in the front row. My aunt leaned over and whispered that they were members of Steve's football squad. Now they were his pallbearers. I asked what position Steve had played. Like a good mother she didn't know, but she knew he was good. (He had been the center for the Hardin Bulldogs.)

As the sermon ended, the preacher read a poem. My uncle began to cry out the same refrain I had heard two days earlier when we had first gone to see Steve lying in the funeral parlor. On that day, my uncle, despite his athletic build, buckled at the knees and had to be supported by two of his brothers as he cried in an anguished voice, "Stevie, Stevie, Why did you do it? Oh my boy, oh my boy!"

No father was ever made strong enough to lose his boy.

Lightning lashing across the Montana sky seemed appropriate on this day. In my mind's eye my uncle has taken on the image of an ancient, agrarian prophet, refusing to be comforted or to leave his boy to the fresh-turned soil. I see him still, as clearly as the day I looked back through my rearview mirror, and his cry in my mind has become indistinguishable from the cry of Yahweh for his children: "How can I give you up oh Israel, how can I make you like Adamah? How can I treat you like Zeboiim? My heart recoils within me. My compassion grows warm and tender . . . I cannot for I am God and not man."

But of course, in the end he must, even if the loss is greater than a God can bear.

On an unforgettable day, in the summer of 1970, I learned firsthand what it means for a father to lose a child. It is a horrible sight. A father is angry on a day like that. Certainly, not at the child. Not even at the wrongdoing. But at the loss no father was ever meant to bear. "How can I give you up?"

Glen Greenwalt is a professor of theology at Walla Walla College, where he has taught since 1978. He is a 1971 graduate of WWC.

Hale-Bopp

They said there was a saucer
drafting in the double-stranded
tail. Angels were there to

take them home—angels
could only be celestial.
Messengers of God, trumpeters

of revelation. Here they
walk among us. They guide
us from danger, and remove

ravenous cancer. They hold
the hands of orphans and
cradle the heads of the

dying. Behind the body,
the tail is only gases,
dirt and ice particles. Nothing

else. They stand pivotal,
ears swivelled forward, waiting
the experience of falling.

—*Erik Ulland*

*Erik Ulland is a biology graduate student at Walla Walla College.
He received his bachelor's degree in bioengineering from WWC in
1997.*

Who Prays First?

Loren Dickinson

I can still quite clearly picture Tiffany. She bounced into a beginning speech course one fall in the early seventies—an upbeat, composed, well-mannered first-year student. Her speeches? Clear, fluent, graceful, coherent. Kind of a B+, all-American kid, I mused. But all those fetching qualities set me up for a life-sized shock one Friday evening about 9:00 when she—I think it was she—called, incoherent.

For what seemed like a very long stretch of minutes, she—I think it was she—babbled into the phone in an unknown, unknowable tongue. Eventually I caught on. It was Tiffany. What grew still clearer in the ensuing monologue was that Tiffany was reaching the end of her line.

In her college dorm room all alone and falling into a deep psychological chasm, Tiffany had set up herself to end her life. She had stashed in her room, she confessed, the instruments to cause her life to cease, and cease soon.

"Please stay where you are," I pleaded. She agreed. She would meet me in the dormitory lobby—if I didn't wait too long. I didn't. Within minutes—quicker than I had ever covered that mile to the campus—I burst into the lobby of Conard Hall. Tiffany was waiting. She had calmed a bit by now.

That night began a very long journey for Tiffany. The journey included a burgeoning friendship for all of us—Tiffany, our family, and a sharp psychiatrist who

99

understood her religious moorings.

That was nearly 25 years ago. In the intervening decades, what's happened to Tiffany? She finished college, married, had a family, divorced, and now is well into a successful health-care career.

So why a story about Tiffany? I'll tell you. In countless chats in my office in the old administration building, it was Tiffany who was the first student ever to ask me, "Can we pray?"

I had been teaching for more than a decade, and it's embarrassing to admit that the idea was hers, not mine. "And who prays first?" I usually asked.

But I'm not too embarrassed to tell you that she invited me to begin a practice that I've practiced for decades since that first question. Prayer, in fact, is now apt to break out virtually without provocation in the classrooms in which I appear and in the office I inhabit.

It's no credit to me at all. It is, though, to Tiffany and to the One who inhabits all our lives in and out of the home, the shop, and the hoary halls of ivy.

I must append a postscript. A scant year ago I looked up from my desk to see a demure 18-year-old standing in the doorway. She startled me; she looked faintly familiar. "Hi," she chirped. "You don't know me, but I'm Gini, Tiffany's daughter."

Suddenly I wanted to shout, "Oh, yes, I do know you. And who prays first?"

Loren Dickinson is a professor of communications at Walla Walla College, where he has taught since 1962. This article was originally published in the May 8, 1997 Adventist Review. *Reprinted by permission of the* Adventist Review.

Being Honest with God

Warren Libby

Sometimes I have found myself asking if I do my homework because I want to or because I have to, if I attend a Christian college because I want to or because I have no choice, if I think about God because I want to or because I think I ought to. Although sometimes it is hard to answer such questions straightforwardly, I have found that honesty is an indispensable part of developing the conviction and the motivation to live the Christian life. That may sound all-too-obvious, but let me explain.

I grew up being the good eldest son in a Seventh-day Adventist household. I pulled the grades, I fulfilled my responsibilities, I practiced the piano, I respected and obeyed my parents (most of the time), I went to church. I never really found a reason to step out of that mold.

My last two years of high school brought a new perspective to my life. After attending Adventist schools for ten grades, I enrolled in a non-denominational Christian school, and there I felt very different because of my Adventist beliefs. I felt like I was in the spotlight most of the time, like my actions and words carried weight that I could not measure. I felt responsible to act the part. When I chose not to play basketball because of the Sabbath, it was hard to explain why. We both had theology to support our viewpoints, and I wasn't very outspoken about my church and my faith, partly because I wasn't always sure I was doing the right thing.

I became very self-conscious of how I was perceived

by others. I subconsciously began to hold myself to a standard. Being a perfectionist by nature didn't help matters—I never got it quite right. I was either missing opportunities to witness, or I wasn't sure I said the right thing. I was never satisfied, and God's ideal seemed so far beyond my expectations. I was living under a burden of should's and ought-to's. I was stuck in my identity and bound by my reputation, but inside I didn't know if I wanted to be there or not. In short, I suppose I was haunted by guilt much of the time.

Last year all that changed.

I was a student missionary in El Salvador for a year. Another student, Annalee Bieber, and I were the first student workers to live in this area. As I entered that new environment and tried to deal with the differences in culture, I became even more self-conscious about how I was living my religion. We had no precedent, so my idealistic expectations were my only guide. The difference in language, gestures, and lifestyle all contributed to my worry. I could not read people as easily as I can here. The pressure built as I imagined the blunders I was committing. I felt out of control.

My frustrations came to a head one Sabbath afternoon. Sabbath afternoons were usually pretty laid back, giving me welcome leisure to think. That afternoon I was sitting inside the living room in a floral-patterned recliner, enjoying a mild breeze and trying not to sweat. As the thoughts crescendoed in my head, I decided to do something. I told God I was tired of doing things because I should. I was tired of being motivated by ought-to. I was tired of the pressure. I was tired of not making the standard. I was tired of the mind games I played trying to motivate myself. I wanted to live my life from inner conviction, not as a response to a sense of blinding obligation from outside myself.

I challenged some of my basic assumptions about Christianity. If becoming a Christian meant that Jesus was living out a new life within me, then something basic was wrong with the Christianity I thought I had. I did not feel the peace, the joy, the acceptance that I claimed was the result of knowing Jesus. As I sat in the recliner, I told God straight out, "If You want me to keep at this way of life, if You want me to read the Bible, pray, try to be of service, go to church, and be Christ-like in my relationships, then it's Your responsibility. I'm not going to beat myself anymore. I'm done with that, come what may. If you want me to continue this thing of Adventist Christianity, then You're going to have to motivate me from the inside."

It scared me to talk like that. I felt almost like a traitor, but at the same time it was a freeing feeling to let the control slide out of my hands into His.

Changes did not come like lightning, but from then on my relationship with Jesus has grown deeper and wider. I feel accepted and loved and at peace. Jesus is working Himself into every part of my life and making me a more genuinely happy person. I am now able to be honest with myself and with God about what happens in my life.

He listens to me when I'm mad and feel like swearing, when my feelings are hurt, when I'm confused. When I don't feel so Christian, He is there. He is not going to drop me when my emotions change. Because I know He is unconditional, it is more natural for me to bring my thanks and gratitude to Him. I know He cares about me no matter how I feel.

I have a certainty born of experience. I can now tell you with confidence that I choose to be an Adventist Christian. I choose to be at Walla Walla College. I choose to let Jesus be my Savior and partner in life. Freedom is real, and we find it in Jesus.

Warren Libby is a humanities major at Walla Walla College. This article was originally presented at the WWC student week of prayer, January 1999.

Runaway Girl

Delona Bell

It wasn't the first time in my life I'd heard the words.

"Dad and I are on the way to the doctor's office. They have the tests results back, and they want to see us." I'd worked in health care long enough to know that the news wasn't going to be good.

"I'll be right there," I said.

Within an hour, we learned that dad had lymphoma. The adrenaline shot through me, and cloaked in my older daughter garb, I made plans. Soon I had both of them booked on the next flight out to a university medical center, where dad would undergo more tests.

It wasn't the first time, and I could not know if it would be the last. Twenty years ago, my mother called me out of high school history class to tell me we would be taking my nine-year-old brother to Portland for brain surgery. The scenario replayed itself wearily in my head. I imagined the worst.

"Mommy," my 7-year-old son looked up at me. "Is pappa going to die?"

I cannot lie. "Everyone dies sometime," I said in some cerebral search for meaning.

He began to cry. "But he's my favorite," he whispered, almost afraid to speak the words.

We held each other, tears flowing down both of our cheeks. Tears because I knew he was his favorite. Tears because he deserved to grow up with a grandpa.

The night was dark and long. I slept fitfully, waking and tossing, then sleeping, only to be awakened with a jolt.

I wanted to run away, but there was nowhere to go.

All of my life I have looked for ways around obstacles. I have refused to take no for an answer. But now I was stopped where there was nowhere to go but through.

In my earlier years, I would have argued with life. With God. I would have run, insisting that this wasn't fair. But I had also learned the hazards of that journey, and as strongly as the impulse was to go, I knew I had to stay.

Though I knew God could heal my father, I had also given up on the notion of knowing when, or how, God would work. With Job, I could only listen to the power of His claim, "Where were you when I laid the foundations of the earth?"

"Please God," I prayed into the darkness. "I don't have the strength to do this. I'm not ready to say goodbye. I long for my children to have a grandfather. Please God, give me peace."

I cannot tell you how it happened, for to me, it was a miracle as big as parting the Red Sea. There, in the face of uncertainty, fear, loss, I felt—peace not to be confused with an assurance of healing, but an assurance that God would carry us through this dark place.

It is hard to say what the greater miracle is. A healing of the body? Or a healing of the soul?

This was written before my father faced treatment for his cancer, when the outcome was uncertain. At the time I wrote this, I did not believe my father would be alive today. The event was over three years ago. Dad is doing well. We are grateful.

Delona Lang Bell, a 1979 graduate of Walla Walla College, writes from Walla Walla where she and her husband, Michael (WWC 1980), and their two sons live.

The Gift of Life

Rod Bagley

When I turned five, I got a brand new Tonka Truck for a birthday gift. It was a big car-carrier semi-truck. That Tonka was special because we didn't often get new toys. I took special care of that truck, and except for the Donald Duck sticker plastered on the windshield as a driver and a few minor scratches, that truck—23 years later—still looks almost brand new.

In my lifetime, I've received many other gifts: Christmas, birthday, Valentine, and many other presents; at times, gifts from girlfriends, sometimes the kind I'd rather not receive, especially when they're accompanied by a "Dear John" letter. Most of these gifts haven't stayed as well-preserved as my Tonka truck.

One special gift I've received is something we have all received—the gift of life. It is a gift that I have received at least twice so far in my life. The first time was when we all receive it, at birth. The second time I was lying on the ground staring up through a grove of gently swaying pine trees, looking at a beautiful, deep blue sky. The irony was, I had just hit a tree at about fifty miles an hour on my motorcycle. I was lying there with a bone sticking out through my glove, my shoulder was broken, both my lungs were punctured from numerous broken ribs, and my neck was broken in two places. To top it all off, the impact had given me a bloody nose, and I was choking on my own blood. I couldn't move to do anything about it. I knew there was a really good chance I would die.

The first thing that came to my mind was a prayer. I simply said, "Dear God, please don't let me die, and help the ambulance to get here quick." He answered the first part of that prayer positively. He gave me a gift again—life.

As a Seventh-day Adventist Christian, I believe in a God who has an active role in our lives. I also believe that God wants the best for all of us. Yet I've had difficulty integrating this image of God with the realities of living in a sinful world that takes so much away.

One problem with merging a giving image and the reality of losing is the question, "Why?" Why, if God wants to give us everything, does He allow the taking away part? We all understand the ultimate reason. SIN. But that does not explain the details. That does not explain why things go wrong, why we lose loved ones, why we do not get what we desperately want. That does not explain why in a split second my life changed. One moment I was an overly active 20-year-old, young and in love with a wonderful, very beautiful girl. I was someone who had his life planned and knew where he wanted to go. The next thing I knew I was lying in a hospital bed dealing with being paralyzed for the rest of my life and also realizing I had messed up a relationship I thought would last a lifetime. I found myself asking the questions, Why did this happen to me? What did I do to deserve this?

I spent a long time struggling with those questions, more than just the 8 1/2 months I spent in the hospital. I never did figure out "why." To this day I don't know why. I came to realize that for me, there is no answer to those questions. I soon realized that if I kept wondering I'd drive myself insane—literally.

But, do we have to know why for God to be able to take each of our situations and make something good out of it? For me, one cool thing that came out of my situation is that my sister met one of my friends while I was in the hospital. They are married now, and I have an awesome three-year-old nephew: he likes Tonka trucks and cars.

When I got my second gift of life, God also left me with the ability to enjoy that life, which I try very hard to do. I still play with Tonkas, only now they are the kind that weigh 2000 pounds, and I drive them around in an arena and smash into other people! I've won more than one Demolition Derby. I still go four-wheeling, too.

I can't claim that because of my experiences I've got it all together. I don't. I still have questions, and at times—even though I know it's not a good idea—I catch myself wondering why. I find inspiration in Isaiah 40:31: "They that wait upon the Lord shall renew their strength; they shall mount up with wings as eagles; they shall run, and not be weary; and they shall walk, and not faint."

We all have problems and questions in our lives. We're all affected by the reality of loss. While this text in Isaiah is a comfort for life here on earth, it also points us toward the ultimate gift God offers us, eternal life. It will solve our problems, answer our questions, and return our losses. It is as easy to receive as a five-year-old boy joyfully accepts a brand new Tonka. The only way we can't get it is if we don't accept it.

Rod Bagley is a 1999 history graduate of Walla Walla College. This article was originally presented at the WWC student week of prayer, January 1999.

Bless Your Heart

Sheila Meharry

Looking into the empty stare of my mother's face made me wonder what good could come from this experience. If "All things work together for good to them that love God," I now questioned, how could this "thing" called Alzheimer's bring any good? Knowing that God does not create suffering, I wondered, how could an all-loving God make any sense from such suffering?

With my mother, I had gone through the living hell of the confusion and disorientation, of her not knowing me, my brothers and sister, or my dad—the man she had lived with for close to 40 years. And now she lay wasting away in a bed not of her own choosing, in a facility where she had always said she would never go. We had kept mom at home for the first 12 of the 15 years of this dreaded disease. Dad aged horribly during 10 of those 15 years. Since I was the only sibling living in town, I would spell dad so he could take a breather now and then. Two and a half years after the doctor told us we needed to put mom in a nursing home, we finally did. This was the hardest thing dad ever had to do. He loved mom dearly, and while it was draining him financially ($6,000 a month) he held fast to the promise he made God during those vows some 40 years earlier.

Being an independent sort, I never had the need to rely heavily on anyone else, not even my mother. I could not remember ever sitting on her lap. I was just too busy to need any affection, or so I thought. We never hugged or said the "I love you" phrase that is now on my lips almost daily with my own boys. I had arrived at this point in my adult life without ever telling my mother I loved her.

One day I went to visit my mom at the nursing home just after my younger brother left. Someone had given mom a doll that she clung to dearly, day and night. When I arrived that day, I saw that the doll's arms and legs were torn away from its body. At first I could not figure out why mom would do this. Then it occurred to me that with Alzheimer's disease there are what I call "waves," where the afflicted person comes in and out of knowing who a visitor is but has no speech or cognition to respond. My guess was that her baby (my brother) had gone in and had spoken some words of love, and because she was not able to respond as a mother would, she became frustrated to the point of ripping whatever she had in her hands. By the time I arrived, the "wave" had passed and my presence went unnoticed. I could only imagine her frustration at being trapped in a living body with a dying mind.

On a day very close to the end, I stood beside mom's bed. She looked pitiful, not at all like the robust, beautiful mother I'd grown up with. Tears streaming down my face, I said the words that had been so difficult in years past: "I love you mom." Right at that point her eyes focused on mine (it had been months since I had seen any focusing), and she said in a smooth, steady voice, "Bless your heart."

I had come faithfully to this nursing home every other day to visit my mom. Since mom could not communicate in any way, I mainly wanted her to hear my voice and know that I was there. So I would visit with her roommate, who was afflicted with multiple sclerosis. I had become well acquainted with this woman, and knowing her helped me realize that this thing called "suffering" could be eased just by a warm touch of a hand and a kind smile upon a face. I never would have known without mom being there. Would I have ever told mom I loved her, without her being there?

At this same time, one of my husband's relatives was also dying of Alzheimer's. One day, several family members were talking at the dinner table about how horrible the disease is and how, since there is no cure, there should be a law permitting euthanasia so we could put this poor, suffering person out of her misery.

I probably would have agreed easily if I had not just had this experience with my mother. I realized that my mother was suffering much less than her care givers.

I read a passage in a Bible commentary that helped me put my own experience in perspective: "One of the apparent tragedies of life is that those who do the most in the cause of righteousness are those who also suffer the most. The reason may not always be understood. But there is comfort in the thought that Jesus, the sinless One, suffered more than any child of humanity will be called upon to suffer. The servant is not greater than his Lord" (*SDA Bible Commentary* 2:823, No. 2). These words remind me that not only will I not suffer as much as Jesus did, but also that mother did not suffer to that extent either. God knows our limitations on suffering. We think we do, but He's the One who made us. Had euthanasia been administered to my mother when I thought she had gone through enough pain and suffering, I never would have experienced what I did in those last few days.

I started praying for an end three days before mom died. I am a more compassionate person because of what my mother went through. I understand that with faith in God I can endure all things. Mom had 72 years on this old earth. I plan on having about 90. Big deal. The few years we "live" or "suffer" on this planet are nothing compared to what God has planned for us forever. God took what Satan had devised and used it to teach me about compassion. God did bless my heart.

Sheila Meharry is the media technician at Peterson Memorial Library, Walla Walla College.

Amazing Grace

Alden Thompson

It was still some 700 years before Christ. And though David's descendants still ruled as kings, the glitter had long since departed. Those who followed David and Solomon on the throne were mostly a lackluster bunch. Some were downright evil. But there were exceptions. One was Hezekiah.

There seems to be no good reason for Hezekiah to turn out right. His father Ahaz had made a royal mess of things; when he died, the people wouldn't even bury him in the royal tombs.

Maybe Hezekiah's mother, Abijah, played the key role in the spiritual formation of her son, nurturing in him the precious knowledge of Israel's God. But however it happened, the Lord had blessed, for in Hezekiah's day He sparked a revival, the likes of which Jerusalem hadn't seen since the days of Solomon. The story is told in 2 Chronicles 29-30, a story of God's bending the rules to make good things happen.

Now someone as clever as God should know how to make rules that don't need to be bent. Or that can't be bent. In fact, for most of us, God is more than just the maker of "the rules"—He is "the rules."

So what does He do with unruly creatures? Smash 'em? Burn 'em? Nuke 'em? Or does he find some way to save them—perhaps by bending the rules? Precisely. And Hezekiah's story is about God's eagerness to do just that.

Now that may seem surprising, for the God of the Old

Testament has a reputation. He rattles mountains, strikes down rebels, sends out the bears to maul disrespectful boys. (And the stories aren't just imaginary; they really are there!) That's why many gentle Christians avoid the Old Testament; it simply hurts too much to read it.

Hezekiah must have known all the hard stories too. Scripture says he was worried about the "fierce anger" of the Lord. Maybe fear drove him into the work of reform the moment he became king. In any event, he re-opened the temple, repaired its doors, and commanded the priests to clean out the "filth."

Excitement rippled through the city. Good things were happening and the passover was coming. Israel was returning to the God who bore them on "eagles' wings" from slavery in Egypt.

But the calendar was relentless. Hezekiah desperately wanted to celebrate the passover and to celebrate it right. But could they get ready in time? He gave it all he had. So did the workmen. But the priests—of all people, the priests—were dragging their feet.

By the sixteenth day of the first month, everything was scrubbed, clean, and sanctified. But alas, it was too late, two days too late for the passover. According to the rules and the calendar, that great celebration of Israel's deliverance from Egypt fell on the fourteenth day of the month.

Why had the priests been so slow? The people were willing and eager to return to the Lord. Would it be possible to bend the rules and celebrate the passover anyway? It seemed like such a marvelous opportunity. How tragic to be so near and yet so far!

The king huddled with his counselors. Would God Almighty bend the rules? Could they bend them for Him? They decided to try. They would celebrate the passover one month late.

The word went out and the people streamed toward Jerusalem. The city was alive with a spirit of hope and expectancy. The people were hungry for the Lord—and the Lord was doing good things for His people.

But then the rules once more. Many out-of-town guests hadn't prepared themselves properly for the passover. The priests and Levites pitched in to help with the sacrifices. But if the people were to participate fully in the passover, they would have to fly in the face of the rules.

King Hezekiah faced the dilemma squarely. Following the rules was an important part of the reform. But if the people were hungering and thirsting after righteousness, wasn't that longing of their souls more important?

He took the plunge. "Go ahead," commanded the king, "let them worship." And they did, eating the passover "otherwise than as prescribed." They didn't just bend the rules, they broke them.

But Hezekiah was being neither foolhardy nor blasphemous. He had been in touch with God. In the words of Scripture: "Hezekiah had prayed for them, saying, 'The good Lord pardon all who set their hearts to seek God, the Lord the God of their ancestors, even though not in accordance with the sanctuary's rules of cleanness.'"

And "the Lord heard Hezekiah, and healed the people."

Nor was that the last of it. As the worshippers celebrated the passover and the feast of unleavened bread which followed, the renewal of their faith awakened such joy and gratitude that they decided to bend the rules again—and extend the feast for another seven days.

Incredible. Unprecedented. "Since the time of Solomon son of King David of Israel there had been nothing like this in Jerusalem."

If that's what happens when God bends the rules, may He bend them to His heart's content!

But should we? Hezekiah did. Cautiously. Prayerfully. The result was a great blessing to God's people. In actual fact, bending the rules was a first step toward taking God and God's rules more seriously.

Is there a glimmer of hope in your heart, a longing to walk with Him but the rules seem insurmountable?

Don't wait to put your house in order. The king's invitation is in your hand. Head for Jerusalem. Now. Plant your feet on the road to His kingdom and God will move heaven and earth to help you. He'll even bend the rules in order to bring you home.

(Scripture quotes are from the New Revised Standard Version.)

Alden Thompson is professor of biblical studies at Walla Walla College, where he has taught since 1970. He graduated from WWC in 1965. "Amazing Grace" was published as "A God Who Bends the Rules" in the November 1985 Signs of the Times.

A Spiritual Journey

Janice Dopp

A four-year-old child, stretched out on a dark, hard pew, listens to a voice drone on . . . and on . . . and on. Soon the child drowses, oblivious to the droning and the cold, hard pew. The child sleeps peacefully until the organ thunders the postlude. Rubbing sleepy eyes still unwilling to open in the harsh overhead light, the child struggles upright, yawns, and whispers, "Are we going home soon, mommy?"

I relived this childhood memory a couple of years ago when I visited the Portland neighborhood where the stone church still stands. Perhaps the pews are no longer dark, and hard, and cold. But this is the way I remember them—and the beginning of my spiritual journey.

My mother was a seeker of truth. She found the preaching too modernistic at the stone church with the dark, hard pews, and she moved on. Eventually, she became the organist at a very large, prominent church downtown.

I still remember some of the songs I loved to sing in this very large church, but one was a special favorite:

> One door and only one, and yet its sides are two,
> Inside and outside, on which side are you?
> One door and only one, and yet its sides are two,
> I'm on the inside, on which side are you?

Yes, I was happy in this very large church, and I

thought we had found our church home at last. But Mother was still looking.

When I was eleven, my mother and I attended evangelistic meetings. Mother, who had been doing some deep Bible study, responded to the messages presented and was baptized by the evangelist when the meetings closed. Once again I found myself in yet another church—a denomination that held some distinctive beliefs. It was strange, unfamiliar, alien to me.

My dad, a wonderful man, usually attended church with us; but I was impressed that my mother was the leader in spiritual matters. I attended church with her, studied these new truths for myself, and was baptized at age 15 into the church with the distinctive beliefs.

College, marriage, children, ministry followed. The years were busy but rewarding. There were dark moments too: By the time I was 26, both of my parents had died, and I—an only child—thanked God anew for my caring husband, two dear children, and the ever-widening circle of friends we met in our pastoral ministry.

*****

Summer has come and gone. The night air is chilly, suggesting frost. October is a busy time, with outdoor tasks squeezing into shorter days. Tonight I am enjoying a long evening near the crackling fire in my wood stove sitting at the dining room table with a stack of Christmas cards waiting for my penned greetings. It is a huge job, yet I wouldn't give it up for anything.

Each of the cards before me represents an important part of my being—loved ones, friends—warm memories. I hear from many of these special people each year, and I read again their last note or letter before I pen my words. My spiritual journey replays as I read and reminisce.

The scene before me now is Anchorage, Alaska: Christmas Eve exactly 40 years ago. We were pastoring there and busily involved with the annual caroling to raise money for the needy and for our mission school. This was our 14th night of caroling. The -40° F. air was too cold for live, outdoor singing, so we broadcast the carols from speakers on top of our car and walked door to door through squeaky snow. The scene was Christmas-card perfect: beautiful white flakes floating down with no wind. Christmas Eve was my favorite caroling night—people's hearts were so warm and open to giving.

The card I'm holding is addressed to someone I've kept in touch with ever since that Christmas—a woman we had the privilege of baptizing during our ministry in Anchorage. Last year she wrote: "I'm so pleased we have stayed in touch all of these years. . . . I enjoy hearing from you and think of how wonderful it would be to see you and have a nice visit."

*****

The yard and garden are trimmed and plowed, and the last of the day-neutral strawberries await picking. It is early November, and my Christmas greetings are progressing well. I pick up a card from the stack before me. Inside the envelope flap, I have tucked in the last year's greeting—a touching collection of pictures and personal notes. One particular enclosure catches my eye: "And God shall wipe away all tears from their eyes. . . ." These words from a memorial service program are a reminder of a husband's loss—his dear wife—and my good friend.

She was a superb musician. I remember a very special Christmas trip in Austria 27 years ago with her Christian youth singing group. It was an unforgettable mix of youth witnessing through music and skiing in the Austrian Alps. None of us will forget our friendship with the Austrian family who managed the small hotel we filled.

My thoughts return to the task at hand. I ask God to

guide my words to comfort and encourage this bereaved man. My husband had performed their wedding in a long-ago December. Checking the wedding file in the study, I find a copy of the marriage license. It is dated December 21— exactly 23 years before the date of this memorial service.

*****

November is swiftly slipping by, and my stack of cards shrinks. It's a good thing, as I want to finish them by Thanksgiving and prepare the printed letter with general news for everyone. When December rolls around, I like to enjoy the holiday programs and family traditions that make the Christmas season special, so December 1 is my goal for mailing all 263 cards.

I glance at the name on this next card. The fact that I even know this family is a marvel. I embrace them in my memory as I recall our first meeting over seven years ago. We owned a piece of vacation property in Northwest Washington, where we spent a few weeks in late summer. This year the rain drove us to the Canadian Sunshine Coast—the name sounded inviting. With our sleeping bags and provisions in the back of our covered pick-up, we ferried to the Sunshine Coast and found better weather.

After our first night out, we decided to travel north and find a nice spot for breakfast. Soon we were following a slow car that tempted us to pass. Since we weren't in a great hurry, though, we stifled our impatience. How fortunate! The car turned into a picnic area, and we followed. A young couple stepped out of the car, and we started visiting. We were so compatible they seemed like old friends. They were taking a few days away from their busy dairy farm where grandma was caring for their two young children. Later in the day we saw them again after a hike along the coast. As we visited after our hike, I glanced at my watch and could not believe that an hour had passed. We traded addresses and promises to visit again.

We thought of them that year at Christmas time and exchanged greetings. That trip to the Sunshine Coast came to mean a lot to me, as it was the last summer vacation my husband and I had together before his terminal illness descended the following year. By the next Christmas, he was gone.

What a joy it is to hear from this family each year. They are fine, Christian people, and their family has grown from four to seven. I treasure their friendship and the memory of the trip we enjoyed together. I am amazed that this busy mother always takes time to send me a personal note. I'm hoping that one day my family and I can visit these warm, friendly people.

Every year there are new stories. My Christmas correspondence is nearing the half-century mark, and I know that I have grown spiritually through this annual time for reflection and sharing. Since those days when I sang about "one door" to heaven, I have seen my friends travel many paths to reach that door, Jesus Christ, our "Forever Friend." What comforting assurance that is. And while our earthly friendships and relationships cannot go on forever, we can look forward to renewing many of them in the earth made new—as we continue our spiritual journey throughout eternity. I hope to meet you there.

Janice Dopp is the secretary to the Director of Planned Giving at Walla Walla College. She attended WWC from 1947-1950.

All Winter

All winter you studied for this
Spring's seasonal flowers, for perennial colors,
and you rejoiced over the catalogue that named,
completely, the genus and species,
and said to yourself "oh" and "just wonderful"
and felt each warm day was a certainty
that nothing would freeze out there
again, that in your paint-covered, mustard-
colored jeans, you'd get down on your knees
and promise the ground your fidelity too,
and you'd be shining. I have thrilled
to you. I have become a new lover.
I will spend all this spring planting, all
summer watering, all fall covering,
encouraging, protecting, all
winter learning the next garden's words,
dreaming of you, out there on the ground
kneeling and saying "wonderful."

—Dan Lamberton

Dan Lamberton is a professor of English at Walla Walla College,
where he has taught since 1981. He is a 1971 graduate of WWC.

Spring Quarter

I have penetrated to
    those meadows
    on the morning of
    many a first spring day,

jumping from hummock
    to hummock,
    from willow root
    to willow root,

when the wild river valley
    and the woods
    were bathed in so pure
    and bright a light

as would have waked the dead . . .
    There needs no stronger
    proof of immortality.

All things must live
    in such a light.
    O Death, where was thy sting?

O Grave, where was
    thy victory, then?

Henry Thoreau, *Walden*

Good Friday

Adam stirs,
Emerging from His dusty hand
And leans in reverie
Against a Tree he does not understand.

God sees the man, the Tree.
God sees himself a Man upon a tree.
This Friday He's created Calvary.

Mid first-week anthems
Soaring through celestial halls,
He hears a cradle creaking,
Smells a cattle stall,
Sees a soldier shove a stone
Against a marble wall.

With his beginning and His final Word
("Let Adam and the garden be")
God plants the cross forever
Eden's one essential Tree.

—*Carolyn Shultz*

Carolyn Schultz is a professor of English at Walla Walla College, where she has taught since 1970. "Good Friday" was published in Christianity and Literature *32.3 (Spring 1983).*

God and I Meet in a Room

Shanna Hayward

I enter a room. On the outside of the door a plastic engraved sign says "prayer room." A dormitory prayer room seems like a good place to write a paper on the existence of God. I open the door. It swings shut slowly behind me. The pressurized hinge hisses before I hear a quiet click.

I breathe in Adventist air, the smell of stagnation, and a heavy burdened feeling reminds me I am supposed to pray. I am guilty. Two low chairs greet me and offer me a seat. They remind me of two old men talking of outdated church controversies and the sins of the human race. They are perfect—no rips mar their surface and they are still shiny as if they were made yesterday.

The only mark of age lies in their style, one 70s orange, one 50s green.

The chairs seem to corner a small table covered with a haphazardly placed tablecloth crumpled up against the hospital-white, painted brick wall. A little basket of plastic flowers and pink ribbons decorates its top. Two *Adventist Reviews* lie nearby. The two old chairs wait knowingly for the table to convert, to give up its tableness and be a chair like them.

I try to imagine the presence of God in this prayer room. If a room reflects a way of life, a way of viewing God, I could not come to believe in God here. This stuffy room reminds me of the stale perfection that many believe is the true path to God.

Funny how such a room can make me so sleepy. . . . I have fallen asleep. I am going back to my own room, distracting but real.

Maybe I can let some nature in through the window to keep me awake.

I come into my own room. I notice a visitor sitting at my desk, philosophizing: We can only see God through our own humanity, our own human qualities. We, like those two "old men" in the prayer room, see only the world we live in. Who is God but what we imagine Him to be?

Hmm. Yes, I believe you are correct, I answer. I cannot reach God or fully understand God through my own mind, through my own experience and human understanding, but I do believe certain ways of living life leave a way open for God to reach me and for me to understand parts of Him.

I see rooms as ways of life. Rooms are like realms of understanding. The prayer room is one realm of understanding. This is the world of those two unchanging old chairs. It is a room that contains no mystery. There are no windows to the outside. There is no reason to ask questions (there is nothing to ask about). The door is shut. I know of different realms with open windows, fresh air moving in and out, and a door I have the choice of leaving open if I like.

A room I love to be in is my room at home. My room at home changed periodically.

Often my Sabbath activity was rearranging it or cleaning it. While rearranging my room, I discovered things that I had forgotten about. Many times I did not even finish rearranging the room, but left it. One time a *National Geographic* caught my interest. I spent the afternoon drawing a red-clothed Buddhist boy lit by an invisible fire. I pondered his room, his world and his God.

My room disappeared for the time I spent with him. Cleaning my room was only a means of discovering the old treasures out of which to make new treasures like the painting of the boy.

Recently, I painted my room a green—not a dull green like the 50s chair in the prayer room, but a fresh green— new like crocus shoots in springtime. My mouth waters when I see the color, for it reminds me of something I can bite into and quench my thirst.

The two corners of the green walls hold my treasures. My dad built me bookshelves in one corner. They are old-fashioned, built-in shelves. The books have helped form my life—my beliefs, thoughts, and philosophies. Children's books take up the first and second shelves. *Ramona the Pest*, *The Last Battle*, and the Laura Ingalls Wilder books (a series I have yet to finish), eye me. They scream at me: "Hey, remember us? We taught you of freedom, of the divine, of creativity, and the need to know the real." Other shelves shout at me for attention—books on crafts, herbal medicines, farming, alternative lifestyles. Plato, Aristotle, Aristophenes and other ancients swing their legs over one shelf and ask questions. They taught me to ask questions, too. German books, diaries, cookbooks, school books: These are reflections of my philosophies, my ideas, my thoughts.

These have been my education.

These books symbolize an upbringing, a philosophy, a view on life, many rooms to see out from. I believe each person's room I enter teaches me to see God in another way. Since I must view God through my own understanding and experience, I say, let that experience be broad, so I can see the most aspects of God possible.

If the bookshelves symbolize the education I have had, the old traveling chest in the opposite corner symbolizes experience and mystery. Its smell of misty sea air and dried flowers lightly fragrances the room. It is a dark, mysterious green color, contrasting and complementary to the young green walls. It stands open. The drawers contain a variety of items such as letters, tins full of feathers, pen nibs, ink, paper, beads, fireworks—items of childhood memories, tidbits that still have potential to be things that let me imagine. The chest contains mystery and story.

The old green chest complements the young green walls. The young green is full of wonder and questions. It is eager to learn all the mysteries the old green chest has to offer. A brown, peeling sticker on the chest states it is from Sweden. But how can the young green walls ever understand the old chest's journey across the ocean from Sweden? They can never know the feel of ocean spray or the smell of fish and sweat on the ship crew as the old green chest did.

My relationship with God is like the relationship between the young green wall and the old green chest. God contains many mysteries I can open up and discover. He gives me things out of which I can make my own creations. Words label Him just as the sticker on the old chest says "Sweden." But I can never know where God comes from or why He is there.

As I lay in the "prayer room," I wondered if there was a word in English for someone who prays. All I could think of was "pray-er." But "prayer" is the act of praying. Perhaps I am a prayer. I live a prayer.

I will live my prayer in my green room, fresh and new, smelling of outdoors, dried flowers and mystery, surrounded by the prayers of Aristotle and Socrates, of *Ramona the Pest* and C. S. Lewis, my green wall and my deep green travel chest. How can I not pray?

Shanna Hayward is a 1999 art graduate of Walla Walla College.

We Have This Hope

Jill Lamberton

One of the keenest memories I have of my year as a
student at the *Colegio Adventista de Sagunto* is my first
Sabbath worship service in the school's sanctuary. This
sanctuary also served as forum for evening worships,
Saturday night videos, student or faculty talent shows,
drama class performances, and music practice. The
sanctuary was multi-functional out of necessity: It was the
largest room on the campus. At first, I found holding non-
religious programs in the sanctuary rather sacrilegious, but
soon I came to see it differently. I found the fact that I had
watched secular videos, laughed at suggestive jokes, and
worshiped Sabbath mornings all in the same room a
beautiful thing, a strange but powerful metaphor. It
challenged me, I think. For it seemed right that every
activity the people of God hosted or participated in could
take place in a house of God, though this concept was as
foreign to me as the land where I had come to study, as
foreign as the language of the services and events.

I had come to the school in Spain knowing less
Spanish than many of my fellow American students, and
the first few months of school were especially painful
because I didn't understand a word of conversation or
instruction. As I watched the preacher that first Sabbath
in Spain, I had the comforting sense that I'd heard his
sermon a dozen times before, given by a score of ministers
who spoke my own language. Even though, in my own
country, I had often rolled my eyes in church thinking,

"not this one again," I found it reassuring that the sermon in a foreign language was so familiar. The service closed with a photocopied hymn pasted into the hymnals, and though my favorite part of any worship service anywhere is the hymn singing, I couldn't pronounce the words fast enough to keep up with the music. Though I didn't know it that first day, I would have another chance to get it right. I would sing that same hymn every Sabbath I worshiped there, for it was always the closing hymn in this particular Spanish church. *Una esperanza que todos tenemos es la venida del Señor.*

My final Sabbath in Sagunto, days before I would fly back to the United States to begin my senior year at Walla Walla College, I could hardly sing the words to this now very familiar hymn. This time my difficulty was not due to a language barrier, but to tears. The hymn was by now associated for me with the people of the Sagunto church and with the familiarity of worshiping there, and this was my last chance to sing with them. So, with cracking voice, I sang: *Cuando el tiempo acabe ya los creyentes reiran, cantaran y gritaran: aleluya, Cristo es Rey!*

Several months, maybe a year later, I was sitting with my sister in the Walla Walla College church one Sabbath morning. We opened our hymnals to Hymn 214, one I was unfamiliar with. Together we began singing, "We have this hope that burns within our hearts, Hope in the coming of the Lord." I looked at my sister incredulously and she nodded her head as if to say, "You mean you didn't know this was an English hymn?" Then, without speaking, with knowing and defiant smiles, we continued in unison, *"Tenemos fe que solo Cristo imparte, fe in sus promeses e en su amor"* as the church congregation sang on in English. I didn't care; the hymn, for me, was meant to be sung in Spanish. It just sounded better. To this day, whenever Hymn 214 is chosen for an American worship service, if my sister and I are in church together, we belt out the Spanish words, partly in an attempt to embarrass our minister father, but mostly because we cannot hear the tune of the hymn without being transported to the church community we both worshiped in for one year. "We have this hope, this faith, and God's great love. We are united in Christ. We have this hope that burns within our hearts. Hope in the coming of the Lord."

*****

A few weeks ago, I sat in a chapel service at the Seventh-day Adventist high school where I teach English. A student leader stood up to give a reading and prayer. He said, "I'm gonna read a poem and I'm not really sure who wrote it, but try to listen for its meaning and think about how it can help us be better Christians." Curious about this obscure poem, I prepared to hear something from a Hallmark card or selected from *Ideals* magazine. Then the reader began, "Deathbenotproud thoughsomehave called, call-ed . . . thee . . . Mighty and dreadful, for thou aren't so."

During lunch, a fellow teacher stopped by and said, "I just wanted to drop in and make sure you weren't too depressed that he didn't know John Donne was the author of 'Death Be Not Proud.'" I laughed and told my colleague that actually I was feeling rather pleased because, though the reader didn't know much about the famous poem, I suspected he'd been given it by one of my students who had just studied the poem in my class. I was relieved to know somebody had been listening; one is never sure with teenagers.

On the day we had discussed "Death be not proud," I remember being struck by the power of words so old. Why was it that in a room of 17-year-olds I was moved with goose bumps while discussing a poet whose work was "too King James-sounding" for teenagers? "Death, be not proud, though some have called thee / Mighty and dreadful, for thou art not so; / For those whom thou think'st thou dost overthrow / Die not, poor Death, nor yet canst thou kill me." Students initially weren't sure how to take this poem.

I watched their puzzled faces. For the most part, they glanced down, hoping I wouldn't call on them. Then, in one of those addicting classroom moments, some students looked at the poem with clearing eyes, and a few even dared to make eye contact with me. One student, who had recently lost a close family member, began by reading, "Thou'art slave to fate, chance, kings, and desperate men, / And dost with poison, war, and sickness dwell," and then he explained, "Well, if you're death, you have to hang out with desperate people, you have to hang around with poison and war. So death is really a pretty weak guy."

By the time we made it to the end of the poem, "One short sleep past, we wake eternally, / And death shall be no more; Death thou shalt die," we were talking about hope. What does it mean to trust that Death "shalt die?" Is it true?

Paul writes in Romans, "For in hope we were saved" (Rom. 8:24, NRSV). I am fascinated by this. What does it mean to be saved in hope? In grace, sure. In faith, sure. In hope? As a student of literature, I insist upon the imaginary. And as a member of the Christian church, a person of faith, I insist upon the importance of things unseen yet understood. Paul says, "Now hope that is seen is not hope. For who hopes for what is seen?" (Rom. 8:24, NRSV). A people who accepts and lives the story of Jesus Christ is a people united in a vision, committed to a vision, and that vision is driven by hope.

To hope, I think, is to refuse to accept pain and death as reasonable or permanent. Paul writes to the Ephesians, "I pray that the God of our Lord Jesus Christ, the Father of glory, may give you a spirit of wisdom and revelation as you come to know him, so that, with the eyes of your heart enlightened, you may know what is the hope to which he has called you . . ." (Eph. 1: 17-18, NRSV). We who believe are called to hope, and this is a hope seen with the enlightened eyes of the heart. Hope, then, enables us to see pain with the eyes of the heart, to acknowledge that suffering is real . . . that it is wrong.

*****

The summer after my fourth year of college, one year after I'd sung the Spanish hymn for the last time, I attended two services within a period of three days, one held in each of the two churches where I grew up. The first church was in College Place, Washington, the second in Loma Linda, California. The first service was a funeral, the second a memorial service. Both were for the same person, my high school English teacher. Something was terribly wrong with the world. This was the first time I had actually felt the strength of death, and I was furious, powerless.

In the Seattle airport, as I was flying from College Place to Loma Linda, I ran into a dear family friend. He, too, was traveling to California and was planning to give the benediction at the memorial service. He said to me, "I'm thinking of reading a poem for the benediction—what do you think?" He handed over the *Collected Poems* of Edna St. Vincent Millay, and I read "Dirge Without Music":

> I am not resigned to the shutting away of loving
>   hearts in the hard ground.
> So it is, and so it will be, for so it has been, time out
>   of mind:
> Into the darkness they go, the wise and the lovely.
>   Crowned
> With lilies and with laurel they go but I am not
>   resigned.
>
> Lovers and thinkers, into the earth with you.
> Be one with the dull, the indiscriminate dust.

A fragment of what you felt, of what you knew,
A formula, a phrase remains,—but the best is lost.

The answers quick and keen, the honest look, the
    laughter, the love,—
They are gone. They are gone to feed the roses.
    Elegant and curled
Is the blossom. Fragrant is the blossom. I know.
    But I do not approve.
More precious was the light in your eyes than all the
    roses in the world.

Down, down, down into the darkness of the grave
Gently they go, the beautiful, the tender, the kind;
Quietly they go, the intelligent, the witty, the brave.
I know. But I do not approve. And I am not
    resigned.

There is something in this poem that sets the record
straight. To live in the world as a person of conscience is to
look at pain and death and say, "I know. But I do not
approve." It seems right to me. Hope, too, looks at pain
and says, "I do not approve and I am not resigned."

A few months ago, I shared this poem with my high
school students. One of their former classmates had
tragically died, and I put this poem on the overhead in a
desperate attempt to assure them, "You don't have to think
that there is anything natural about a 17-year-old dying.
You can disapprove. You can say the best is lost."

*****

What, then, is the nature of our hope? It is unseen.
Hope that is seen is not hope. "But if we hope for what we
do not see, we wait for it with patience" (Rom. 8:25,
NRSV). Though it is a mystery to us, still, "Let us hold fast

to the confession of our hope without wavering, for he who has promised is faithful. And let us consider how to provoke one another to love and good deeds . . . " (Heb 10:23-24, NRSV). We live out our hope in love and deeds. We feel ourselves united in true community when we are united in hope. We are saved in our hope.

Una esperanza que todos tenemos es la venida del Senor. We have this hope that burns within our hearts. Hope in the coming of the Lord. This is a song I sing in Spanish, but the burning hope, my own yearning, is beyond language.

―――――――――

Jill Lamberton is a 1996 English, Spanish, and humanities graduate of Walla Walla College. She teaches English at Portland Adventist Academy, Portland, Oregon.

Orchids and Hope

Verlie Ward

On a warm summer afternoon in January 1967, our family of four stood together on the deck of the English liner the *Arcadia*, waving goodbye to family, friends, and everything familiar. I should have had a sense of adventure about this 21-day voyage to the United States, but I was afraid. Would we ever come home? Would we ever live near my family again? Was America as dangerous as portrayed in the news? What would happen to our children? How far would our $1000 of savings go towards buying a car and furniture for our new life?

The band began to play a familiar tune, and we held tight to the streamers that provided our last connection with those we loved. The words of the song left an indelible message on our minds:

> Now is the hour when we must say good-bye
> Soon we'll be sailing far across the sea.
> While you're away, kindly remember me.
> When you return you'll find me waiting here.

The boat moved out into the deep waters of the Pacific Ocean, and I watched with tear-filled eyes as everything familiar grew dim. The ache in my heart only became heavier as we found our way down to our cabin. And down it was, to "F" deck, the lowest deck on the boat. Down where the engine vibration never stopped, down below the plimsoll line where no natural light could penetrate, down where the air smelled stale, down where I felt like Jonah in the belly of the whale. Our small cabin had a handbasin, four narrow bunks, and barely enough space to walk between them. I wondered how I would keep an active two-year-old and a curious six-year-old occupied for the next three weeks.

My first surprise came when I went to fill the bath with water for the children. I discovered that the water did not lather, and a thick scum formed on top. It was salt water out of the ocean! Then there was the problem of meals. Children were not invited to eat meals with adults. An early session was planned for them, and following that, my husband and I took turns going to the dining room. This ritual consumed much of our day. The cooks, unfamiliar with vegetarian tastes, gave us a steady diet of eggs and, for a special treat, leftover vegetables mashed and bound together with flour and eggs, rolled in bread crumbs, and fried.

As the days passed, we began to look around the liner for places to exercise. The decks invited walking, but the boat's speed guaranteed strong winds. Desperate for fresh air, we secured our coats and hats and firmly held our children's hands as we roamed the decks. Beside the swimming pool and in the lounge we listened to fellow travelers describe their adventures. This was my first long-term encounter with Americans. I listened as they spoke of all that they missed from home, their large supermarkets, air conditioning, comfortable cars and large freeways. I loved the winding country roads, small bakeries, and fruit stores of New Zealand. Why couldn't these people love the things that were different in my country, I wondered. My fears about America and Americans escalated, and I was homesick.

The journey continued and seemed endless. Some days and nights were so stormy that even the stabilizers had to be drawn in to prevent the boat from being damaged. I knew I was in the belly of the whale!

Sometimes I was the only member of the family not dogged by seasickness.

Then one glorious Sunday morning the boat entered a calm harbor on the Hawaiian island of Hilo. When the ground stabilized underneath our sea legs, we took a walking tour. The first thing that caught our attention was the cars. They were huge! Ford Galaxies, LTD's and large Chevrolets did not fit our picture of what a car should look like. We were familiar with Morris Minors and Mini Austins and wondered how the roads could accommodate such huge vehicles. Even worse, they drove down the wrong side of the road. As we walked, we began to absorb the sights and glorious smells: jasmine, bougainvillea vines, gardenias, frangipane, lilies and orchids all bloomed in profusion.

Best of all, we found a name that was familiar to us—a Seventh-day Adventist school hosting a work bee that Sunday morning. When they discovered we were teachers, headed for Union College in Lincoln, Nebraska, they invited us to join them for our first potluck. No food ever tasted so good! We devoured fresh fruits and vegetables and real vegetarian entrees and our first brownies. Above all, we found hospitality. Our new friends were different from the American tourists we had met on the ship. After spending several hours with them, we once again headed up the gangplank for the final part of the journey.

As our little family stood on the deck, watching the final preparations for departure, I heard my name over the loud speaker: "Would Mrs. Ward please come to the bottom of the gangplank?" One of our new friends met me there and placed a spectacular lei of orchids over my head. She also handed me more orchids in full bloom and wished me God's blessing for the rest of the journey.

The voyage was transformed. Fellow passengers asked if we had family on Hilo and we smiled and said, "Oh yes, these are members of our church family—we met them for the first time today." They wanted to know what church we belonged to! The cabin in F deck now held hope for me in the form of a spray of orchids. Those flowers and the gifts of time and food reminded us that we were part of a larger spiritual family and that God would go before us. Even when our plane touched down in Lincoln, Nebraska, in our first snow storm, the biting cold did not invade our hearts, because the long journey from home had become an adventure. The gracious Midwestern hospitality we encountered matched that of the believers on Hilo, and our roots grew deep. This was not to be my last life-changing encounter with orchids, however.

It was Easter and the skies of Berrien Springs, Michigan, had been overcast for days. It was a time of sorrow and loss for me. I wondered how I would face the future. I felt bereft and alone. It was Friday afternoon and I dreaded another long weekend. I noticed a florist's package on the front door step of my home and carefully unwrapped the tissue to reveal a beautiful corsage created with the largest white orchid I had ever seen. Attached to the corsage was a card that bore no name but simply read "I Peter 5:7." I reached for my Bible and read the words "Casting all your cares upon Him; for He careth for you." I wore the corsage to every event that weekend with unquenchable joy. I will always remember those words, now forever associated with white orchids.

I have a picture in my mind of heaven strewn with orchids, and I am sure that there will be a large white orchid growing in my garden as an everlasting reminder of the faithfulness of the Promise Giver.

Verlie Ward is a professor of education at Walla Walla College, where she has taught since 1983.

The Way God Works

Kari Hart

I have been accumulating a picture of God for several years now. When I try to describe it, however, the words are elusive. It works best to begin by describing qualities I have come to believe my God has.

First of all, we are all the same in God's eyes.

About seven years ago, my family and I were flying to visit some relatives. My Dad does a lot of traveling, so on this particular trip his frequent flyer gold card had boosted three of our seats to first class. Having a family of five, who should get the first class seats but the kids, of course. So while my parents, whose seats they rightfully were, sat in coach, my sisters and I sat in first class. Did we think we were in the lap of luxury! We were soaking it up as much as we could, relaxing in the plush chairs, our legs barely touching the floor, our bodies practically disappearing inside the cushions. Of course every once in awhile we would turn around and wave at our parents, who could not even extend their legs. We were high class.

Since my one experience in the front of the cabin, I have often walked by the first class passengers, wondering what they do and what gives them the ability to sit there like peacocks as we coachies are herded like cattle. What makes them first class, anyway? Recently I have come to understand that to God there is no first class or coach. Just because those people sitting in first class could afford it does not mean God loves them any more. In His eyes we are all the same. I know I have sinned probably more than, say, my pastor—but that does not mean God loves me any less. Some of us have a hard time believing that God loves the murderer or rapist the same as He loves us, but when we remember that we have all contributed to His sacrificial death on the cross, we should be thankful for His unconditional love. The ground at the foot of the cross is level. We are all the same in God's eyes.

Next, God so graciously meets us where we are.

I have had the privilege recently to work with a teacher, Donna Coffeen, at the Juvenile Detention Center in Walla Walla as a teacher's aide. I tutor the kids one-on-one. After working there for several weeks I became fairly well acquainted with one of the girls, who shared with me something that made shivers run up and down my spine. She told me that she, like I, had been raised a Seventh-day Adventist, but she started getting in trouble in elementary school. She did all the "right" things as she was growing up, praying and reading a chapter out of the Bible every night. Unfortunately, the trouble she got into led her down a wrong path and she eventually ended up in detention. But she had thought a lot while she was in there and decided that when she got out she wanted to change her lifestyle. When she shared that with the other kids, though, they didn't understand and could only think about how high they wanted to get when they got out. Then she told me that she had started to pray again, that she could really feel God's presence. She knew that God was with her even in Juvy.

God meets us wherever we are.

Finally, we can always show Him our true colors because He knows us better than we know ourselves.

Prayer is a powerful tool. To pray, we do not have to be in a building called a church, on our knees, with head bowed and eyes closed. I've come to the conclusion that talking to God anywhere, anytime, is prayer.

When my heart is heavy, my head is bowed, and my eyes are closed, the tears can easily flow. It happened, for

142

instance, the last Sabbath of Christmas vacation when I was at my home church in Calimesa, California, with my parents. We had just begun the closing prayer in the traditional style when I did the unthinkable: I opened my eyes (I confess I actually do once in awhile, whether to stop the tears or to observe others). I have discovered that you can learn a lot about people while they are praying.

That Sabbath I noticed that many others were similarly wiping tears from their closed eyes. It hit me again how much pain and suffering our world contains. Not only that, but how stoic we human beings try to be when hiding hurt from others. And then my third point came to mind.

As good as we all are at hiding our pain from friends and family, it is harder to do so when we are in prayer with our nonjudgmental God, or when our faces are looking questioningly up to the heavens. None of us should have any fear of showing our true colors to our Creator and friend, as some were doing that beautiful Sabbath morning when I saw them letting their burdens fall away.

Not only can we unashamedly cry as hard as we want in front of Him, we can laugh our loudest and dorkiest laugh as well. He doesn't mind if we yell or scream, or rant and rave. We can even be mellow and He won't wonder why we aren't being our usual bubbly self. He understands each of us completely. We can always show God our true colors because He knows us better than we know ourselves.

I have not come by these images of God through any great spiritual revelation. I've led a pretty ordinary life. No missing keys found in the middle of a park at midnight, no wet wool and dry ground when I've tried to make big decisions, and definitely no lightning. I have tried to test our Creator, but for some reason God hasn't spoken to me in those ways. He has communicated with me in ways that He knows are best: through an ordinary life of searching and faith, through other people and everyday experiences. More often than not, I think, that is the way God works. As I've gathered my images of God they have made me strive even harder to be like Him and to strain to hear that still, small voice.

God is so good, and He wants us all to come to know Him as the best of friends. He is not just about lightning and miracles but more about the simple way of life. In Philippians 4:4-9, Paul writes,

"May you always be joyful in your union with the Lord. I say it again: rejoice! Show a gentle attitude toward everyone. The Lord is coming soon. Don't worry about anything, but in all your prayers ask God for what you need, always asking Him with a thankful heart. And God's peace, which is far beyond human understanding, will keep your hearts and minds safe in union with Christ Jesus. In conclusion, my brothers and sisters, fill your minds with those things that are good and that deserve praise: things that are true, noble, right, pure, lovely, and honorable. Put into practice what you learned and received from me, both from my words and from my actions. And the God who gives peace will be with you" (Good News Bible).

I hope that we don't give up on the search to find that best friend in God. He will speak to each of us in the way He knows we will respond to best. May we all have patience and an open ear to that still, small voice.

Kari Hart is an elementary education major at Walla Walla College. This article was originally presented at the WWC student week of prayer, January 1999.

Temperance

Dan Lamberton

We didn't drink. My grandparents didn't—neither
side. My parents didn't. It was indisputable. No one I
knew well drank anything stronger than Hires. Coca-Cola
and Pepsi were caffeinated and made with bird manure,
my aunt said. Beer was as far off as war, as separate from
me as jail. At school we signed pledges to touch not, taste
not. We carried little cards with our temperence pledge in
our first wallets. We learned that drinking made you
crazy, made you flop around, made you like jazz, made
homes go bad. Because he brought alcohol back, my
grandmother hated Roosevelt. My mother, who believed
in bitter experience, gave us all a warning taste when my
brother and I found a brown bottle of Lucky out in the
sagebrush.

Every year a man in a gray Plymouth drove up to our
two-room school carrying a satchel, a brown paper bag, a
gallon mayonnaise jar, and a cage. From the satchel, he
brought our new pledge cards. This card was my license,
my first official signature, my social security, my safe
driving future. I promised to praise God with my body
and keep my soul clean by not defiling God's temple in
me. The man with the cards was Elder Bowman. He'd
driven from Spokane and he announced that there would
be a film in the 4th to 8th grade room, that night at 7:00.
We were to go.

The film was about a man who smoked and drank
and got cancer. We watched him be cut open. We saw his

defiled lungs and his stained liver. After the film the man from Spokane brought up from the floor the gallon jar, the grocery bag, and the cage. From the grocery bag he drew four large bottles of beer and opened them with a gadget we used for pop. But the beer opened with a softer, more grown-up sound—like a suppressed burp at the table. The beer smelled like cereal gone sour, and it foamed out the tops and ran down the bottles' sides like saliva around a nervous horse's bit.

Elder Bowman took a knife and jabbed a few holes in the jar lid, reached into the cage and pulled out a frog, bigger than any frog I'd ever seen, a frog-leg dinner bullfrog named Buddy. He held Buddy up for us to see, then set him down on the desk and tickled his bottom so Buddy would jump. Buddy was as long as the jar, and Elder Bowman put Buddy into the full jar of beer and closed the lid and let Buddy bubble and struggle and soak until Buddy settled down. Then he pulled the frog out of the jar, held him by one fore-leg and laid him down on the table. He prodded Buddy's sides with his finger and pinched his vestigial tail. Buddy tried to jump but his legs wouldn't work together and we laughed.

Not all the children who'd signed temperence pledges grew up to keep them—but often, seemingly from nowhere, reminders of those past convictions appear in ways that are sometimes dream-like, sometimes as real as heartache, sometimes as weird as can be. Years after Elder Bowman's visits, when our farm pond was filled with peepers, ducks, and algae, there came from nowhere deep brown sounds at night, roars like lions, that sent my parents out to see who was in agony or who was lost and intoxicated out on our farm. And there were the calling bullfrogs, who'd come mysteriously, hardened and secure as lost brothers, to our land.

Dan Lamberton is a professor of English at Walla Walla College, where he has taught since 1981. He is a 1971 graduate of WWC.

The Other Shoe

Shirley Cody

The warm Mississippi afternoon was quiet—a bit *too* quiet. Mothers of small children learn to suspect such peaceful times. When I went outside to check on Carole I found, here and there around the yard, a couple of crumpled socks, one barefoot toddler, and one scuffed saddle oxford. The good one, the one without a hole in the toe. "Where's your other shoe, Carole?" I asked.

"I don't know," she replied indifferently. Shoes were outside the scope of her concerns.

The hunt began—front porch, back porch, under the house, all around the yard. No shoe. My teenage brother came over to visit and was drafted to help search. When my husband came home from work, we all looked everywhere again. Still no shoe.

Carole now offered her only "helpful" comment: "Poochie got it" (Poochie was the pup belonging to the neighbors who occupied the other half of the old house). Well, if Poochie got it he had certainly done a superb job of hiding it!

I took Carole into the house. There was some explaining to do.

"Carole, it's a week until Daddy's payday. You've lost your shoe and we don't have any money to buy you any more. You'll have to stay in the house and wear your bedroom slippers. It's not hot enough to go barefoot yet."

How much of this Carole comprehended is questionable. She did understand the part about staying indoors, though. Tears began to flow. "But I want to go outside!" she wailed.

However, inside she had to stay, a very miserable two-year-old, wearing bedroom slippers.

That evening, several hours after tucking Carole into her bed, I crawled gratefully into my own. I never had any trouble sleeping—usually Carole and her baby brother kept me pretty well worn out most days. But tonight I lay awake. I kept thinking about shoes and money, money and shoes.

My husband and I had both dropped out of college for lack of money (this was before the days of government loans). Since college was the key to better-paying jobs, my husband, with no degree, was starting at the bottom as a computer operator. We were just barely getting by while trying to pay off debts that seemed to us mountainous: college bills and doctor bills for the births of our two children.

Finally, tired out by fruitless worry, I decided to bring my problem to God. In the darkness of our one bedroom, surrounded by my sleeping family, I closed my eyes.

"Father, you know we don't have the money to get Carole any more shoes right now. Please help me find that shoe tomorrow."

That was all the prayer I was able to accomplish before weariness took over and I fell asleep.

Early the next morning, I shuffled sleepily out onto the front porch and pushed open the screen door. Yawning, I bent over to pick up the morning paper. Suddenly my yawn collapsed. There, neatly centered on the front step, complete with the hole in the toe, was one small saddle shoe.

Shirley Cody is the librarian/registrar at the Walla Walla College School of Nursing campus.

Blueberry Toast

Terrie Aamodt

Our American culture is passionate about wine.
People rhapsodize about certain strains of grapes, about
certain combinations of soil and sunlight in France, about
cellars and barrels and bouquets. They name their children
after favorite vintages. I understand their passion only
with my mind, not with my nose or taste buds. I used to
credit that to my childhood membership in the American
Temperance Society or to some innate cultural clumsiness.
Now, though, I know it is because I already am part of a
tradition complete with recipes handed down from
generation to generation and dependent on certain
combinations of soil and sunlight. For me, if we're talking
passion, we're talking blueberries.

Blueberries are not those pallid impostors that lie
bloated and gasping between layers of cardboard and
plastic in the supermarket. If you blind taste-tested
mashed store-bought blueberries and the mashed, juice-
soaked cardboard they came in, you would detect very
little difference. I call them mooshberries. Mooshberries
grow on fat farms where greedy capitalists inject them
with synthetic growth hormones as if they were burger-
bound steers. The only good thing about mooshberries is
that they are so insipid you can mix them half and half
with real blueberries. The real blueberries have an *excess* of
taste, and they storm through their dumpy cousins without
diminishing their own wild flavor—*voila*, twice as many
pies. Real blueberries are wild, and the definitive ones

grow in Alaska. They sweep over your senses and transport you to a wilderness of bears, salmon, eagles, wolves, and frost-tipped red bushes. These berries are exuberant and tangy. When you eat them your tongue tingles, either from their wild tartness or because they evoke a sublime, dangerous place where a grizzly might be devouring berries behind the next bush. Real blueberries are intoxicating.

The Pacific Northwest, between its wild mountain huckleberries in the Blue Mountains and its blueberries on the slopes of Mt. Baker, offers everything Alaska did except the grizzlies. And mooshberries abound for pie-stretching.

We have a family tradition that when you turn 50, or whenever you get tired of counting the candles on your cake, you get a pie instead. The definitive pie is blueberry, and it is ideally served warm but not runny with a scoop of vanilla ice cream to tame it just enough to keep you from fainting with pleasure. Blueberry pie for breakfast is slightly decadent, so we have developed a more practical morning alternative: blueberry toast. In some ways it's better than pie because it's more aesthetic. You can see the blueberries swimming in their rich juice as they spill over a piece of sourdough or 8-grain toast. The rising steam hits your nose just as your mouth starts to water. And you notice that the berries don't look blue at all. Their juice is a deep, rich burgundy. It ought to be displayed in an elegant bottle with just the right backlighting.

One reason blueberries taste so good is that they evoke all the pleasures and hardships of picking them. I'm not very good at blueberry picking. One floundering pass through a bush might yield four berries: two drop on the ground, one gets smashed, and one falls in the bucket. My mother has better picking stories to tell. Once when she was pregnant with me she sat for an hour in one spot and picked a gallon of huckleberries. My father, though, was the undisputed best berry picker. His big, dexterous hands flew through the bushes as clusters of berries leaped off their stems into the pail. He could out-pick any two of us.

It was only fitting that my father was the one who landed on the front page of the paper with an accompanying color photo essay. When he went blueberry picking at a local farm, he just happened to be wearing a red shirt, as he always seemed to be doing when a photographer appeared. The camera picked him up like a magnet. One picture was a closeup of his cupped hands with blue-stained fingers nestling a pile of blueberries. He told the reporter how he grew up in the blueberry-rich Cascades and described his passion for picking them. The only thing more fun, he always said, was baking pies for people.

Blueberries, along with his homemade bread, were part of my father's pastoral ministry. During the summer of 1992, one of his parishioners was immobilized after back surgery. More than anything, my father would have liked to have spoken a word to take away her pain. But he did have a splendid anesthetic within his powers—one of his blueberry pies.

My father was unable to eat blueberry pie himself then. Something was wasting his body and consuming him alive. His once-powerful frame was stooped and skeletal, and for the only time in his life he looked like an old man. No food, not even blueberries, agreed with him. In September he found enough strength to take us on the annual pilgrimage to Mt. Baker to harvest blueberries. Our 18-month-old daughter romped through the rain-soaked brush turning her face purple with berries, and her grandpa once again outpicked the rest of us.

Soon after we came home he was diagnosed with cancer and lived less than 6 weeks. During the dark, snowy months afterward, I can remember every now and then pulling a box of blueberries out of the freezer with his handwriting on it: Mt. Baker '92. And every time we pick berries or eat them now, I remember my father. I believe, though, that our customs, our traditions, and our sacraments are not just about memory, about foods once eaten with an absent loved one or about unleavened bread and wine shared by a small group on a Jewish religious holiday thousands of years ago. They can point ahead as well. When my father gets to heaven he's going to have a ravenous appetite. And when he hurries up to the long table, I won't be surprised at all if he finds his place set with a steaming plate of rich, purplish-red, juicy blueberries spilling over toasted homemade bread. For me, if we're talking passion, we're talking blueberries.

Terrie Aamodt is a professor of English and history at Walla Walla College, where she has taught since 1979. This article originally appeared in the June 16, 1994 Adventist Review. *Reprinted by permission of the* Adventist Review.

Outside the School of Theology

Teri Zipf

Outside the School of Theology, an article
from *The Sun* is taped to the wall.
"Adam & Eve's Skeletons Found—
in Colorado!" The photo shows two

skeletons lying rib by rib. Their knees bend in
the same direction, Adam's in the space
behind Eve's. His right arm—humerus, radius,
and ulna—stretches beneath Eve's head,

her pillow for the night, for forever.
I'm glad to see Adam didn't hold a grudge
about the apple. Of course, a lot has happened
since then. Cast out of the Garden, they

wandered for a while, took up farming.
Maybe when Cain was grown
they bought a Winnebago and crisscrossed
America, sent postcards to the grandkids.

"Overheated in a godforsaken desert,"
Adam would say. "Think I'll call it
Death Valley." He was still in charge
of naming. Finally one day,

they got tired. Or maybe they thought
they had wandered back to Eden.
I've felt that way, in Colorado.
So many years had passed, they had

forgotten about the snake. Eve's
days of childbirth were long
gone and Adam was done scraping
his living from the thin soil of Goshen.

They lay down. They looked
at the stars. They were so old
they no longer thought they could
distinguish good from evil.

They said their nightly prayer
for Abel. Eve said, "Adam, it's time
to go home." And Adam said,
"All right, dear. Good night."

ıf works in new media at Coffey Communications. She
₹ English graduate of Walla Walla College. "Outside
ₗ of Theology" is from her book of the same title,
ᵢved the 1998 William Stafford Memorial Poetry
ᵪ the Pacific Northwest Booksellers' Association.